WHAT OTHEI

THE ETERNITY LENS:

If you read this book it may well change your life. You will discover that living with an eternal perspective in the real world is the most fruitful way to live life. You will walk with Dr. Bill Coleman through real life experiences that have changed the lives of people around the world. I highly recommend it.

- Gary Chapman, Ph.D. Author of "The 5 Love Languages"

I like the ETERNITY LENS by my brother Bill Coleman. First, it is well written and interesting. Bill is a gifted story teller and also quite witty. Second, it will bless, encourage and guide you to see life in the light of the hope of the gospel of Jesus Christ and all that we have in Him. You will enjoy this fine work.

- Dr. Daniel L. Akin, President,
Southeastern Baptist Theological Seminary

In C.S. Lewis's "Screwtape Letters," Screwtape reminds his young demonic protégé that his business is to fix his patient's attention on the stream of immediate sense experience. Teach him to call it "real life" and don't let him ask what he means by "real." In The Eternity Lens, Coleman gently and winsomely draws the reader's attention beyond the stream of sense experience to that which is real, the eternal.

- Dr. Evan Posey, Vice President for Academic Affairs,
Luther Rice College and Seminary

This book gave great encouragement to me. I recommend it as a fundamental piece of reading for believers at all stages of their faith walk. It contains critical, biblical principles for every believer and follower of Jesus Christ, in helping us to understand the "bigger picture" of God's eternal work in our daily lives. It also gives joyful purpose to those difficult moments of adversity that God uses to build up and sharpen our faith and prepare us for eternity.

- Mark Carnes, Lead Pastor, He's Alive Church

"The Eternity Lens" by Dr. Bill Coleman is an engaging book that provides a healthy biblical lens through which all Christians should view life. Coleman masterfully uses stories and humor to reinforce a biblical perspective of eternity and its impact on the way we think and live. It's biblically sound, practically relevant, and I highly recommend every Christian read it and allow God's eternal perspective to become yours here on earth.

- Dr. Kevin Harrison, President
West Coast Bible College and Seminary

Through story of family, sports, bars, missions, humor, international travel, life trials, and more, Bill effectively conveys the reality of the love of God in Christ Jesus. Eternal perspective resonates in my soul, and for that reason, I devoured this book in under 24 hours. Delight in Jesus Christ and His kindness, on display in the Bible. Let the glory of God infiltrate your everything, as you belong to the God who made you and saved you. "The Eternity Lens" will help. I heard most of the Scripture and many of the stories in conversation over coffee or pizza, and on one long (and enjoyable) car ride. I read the whole book in Bill's voice. I attest that his life declares the same Truth his words speak from these pages. Live your life for Christ who loved you and gave himself for you. Love the Lord with your everything. Walk in joy.

- Greg Helms, Missionary to Uganda and Around the World

THE
ETERNITY LENS

Living in the Real World
with an Eternal Perspective

BILL COLEMAN

XULON PRESS

Xulon Press
2301 Lucien Way #415
Maitland, FL 32751
407.339.4217
www.xulonpress.com

Paperback ISBN-13: 978-1-6628-2712-9
Ebook ISBN-13: 978-1-6628-2713-6

Table of Contents

Section 1:
"Though our outer self is wasting away..."

Section 2:
"Our inner self is being renewed day by day..."

Section 3:
"For this light momentary affliction is preparing for us an eternal weight of glory beyond all comparison..."

Section 4:
"As we look not to the things that are seen but to the things that are unseen..."

Section 5:
"For the things that are seen are transient but the things that are unseen are eternal."

A Cautionary Conclusion

ACKNOWLEDGMENTS

THE FACT THAT THIS BOOK HAS TAKEN SO LONG to write means that the number of folks to thank has multiplied over the years. My wife stands at the forefront. I have watched her navigate the role of being a pastor's wife and find her own places to serve within the church, all while holding our family together. Her support and understanding of the demands on my life's mission has been remarkable. I would not be where I am today without her.

My parents have believed in me and my calling since before I took my first breath. Their guidance and support have been used by God to shape me into who I am today. I have had many professors and mentors over the years who fed into me. I am grateful to God for using these individuals to impact my life so that I can better impact others. Since I began this work, I have served in 3 churches: Glenn View Baptist Church, Bedrock Community Church Roanoke, and He's Alive Church. I have been blessed to have such incredible folks to pastor along the way who have provided encouragement and support.

I did my best to not let my kids play second fiddle to the ministry over the years. That said, I am sure there were times and moments that I failed, but their love and devotion to me never seemed to wane. It is to them that I dedicate this book. Austin and Alaina, as you navigate this crazy temporal world, make your unique journeys, and cultivate your own families, may you never cease to see all of life through the lens of eternity. For in the end, that is what matters most.

I am thankful for those who have joined me on this journey. Most people are lucky to have one best friend in life. God blessed me with four (in order of appearance): Jim Johnson, William Wilson, Jackie Watts, and Mark Carnes. The impact these men have had on my life cannot be overstated. Susan Grace gave her incredible talent to creating the original artwork for the book cover. Ann Wayne, Laura Stamey, Kelly Freestone, Alaina Coleman, and Katie Graves were great resources for me in the technical areas of book publication, editing, and promotion. Our Wingate College crew couples have journeyed with us through the years: Carnes, Graves, Sluders, and Svensons.

Finally, but most importantly, all glory for anything of worth that comes out of my life is directed solely to my King: for my salvation, for my calling, for my vision, for my purpose. This work is an offering to You, Lord. Take it and do with it as You wish. It all belongs to You, Jesus. Until our faith becomes sight, we will persevere forward with our eyes firmly fixed on eternity with You.

INTRODUCTION

1 7 YEARS OLD. HEAD IN MY HANDS. EYES PUDDLING up. "God, just tell me what to do."

I remember it like it was yesterday. I had just finished my Junior year of high school. Summer had begun. I was excited for the break and pumped about my senior year. However, I was weighed down by a major decision I had to make that would affect my senior year.

I asked the Lord for some direction, but there was no lightning bolt. The bush outside of the garage did not burst into flames followed by His voice. I did not experience the presence of a dove coming down and God's thunderous declaration from the sky. I had no Mount of Transfiguration encounter. Instead, as He often does, I was drawn to His Word.

As I studied my Bible on a hot, June day in Florida, I had a moment that would forever tattoo itself on my heart. I "just happened" to be reading in 2 Corinthians. When I approached the end of chapter 4, I got blindsided by the truth.

2 Corinthians 4:16-18

So we do not lose heart. Though our outer self is wasting away, our inner self is being renewed day by day. For this light momentary affliction is preparing for us an eternal weight of glory beyond all comparison, as we look not to the things that are seen but to the things that

are unseen. For the things that are seen are transient,
but the things that are unseen are eternal.

After the initial punch to my soul, I read it repeatedly, letting the richness of these words permeate my being. I had been looking at this decision through the wrong lenses. I needed a new perspective. It was at that moment these verses became my "life verses."

Making a list of pros and cons is not a bad process, but that was not going to be sufficient this time. I realized the things of this world we make a big deal about are temporary. Don't misunderstand, their temporal nature does not equate automatically to insignificance; rather they are "preparing us for an eternal weight of glory beyond all comparison."

What happens when we put on the eternal glasses to gain a new perspective? This perspective does not change *what* we see. It changes *how* we see it.

In my scenario, at 17 years old, I came to understand that the process of faith by which I walked was more important than any one decision. There was great freedom in that realization. I had a choice to make between two equally acceptable paths. Either decision could be used for His glory. Neither was specifically prohibited or commanded in the Word. This is where relationship with the Creator is magnified. This is where we understand walking by faith and not by sight—not just intellectually but experientially. I could confidently make a temporal decision and boldly walk into a temporal future because my life was wrapped up in eternity.

As a pastor, I have found so many people who are trapped in the temporal. There are so many ways our eyes get adverted from the eternal. There are worries, heartaches, disappointments, griefs, betrayals, tragedies, and just plain selfishness. I have tried to counsel, encourage, and challenge folks to see thing through an eternal perspective. I certainly do not always see the circumstances around me through those eternal lenses; God has developed that sense in me over the years.

As I have committed myself to an eternal perspective, I have studied and seen this truly is God's perspective as well. It seems everywhere I turn in the Word, the perspective that undergirds all things is an eternal one.

God makes Adam and Eve to live forever. They sin and break relationship with an eternal God. God makes a promise to Abraham to bless the world through his yet-unborn child. Israel is formed and chosen to bring forth a Savior for the world. The eternal Son takes on flesh, born as a baby in the humblest of circumstances. He grows mentally, physically, and spiritually. He calls disciples and engages in 3 years of investing in them through teaching with displays of glory and doing life together. He is arrested and crucified in that historical moment—though the Bible clearly says God knew this moment before the foundation of the world (1 Peter 1:18-20). He rises from the dead to conquer death and hell. His offer is eternal and abundant life to anyone who would believe. Sinful people cannot inherit the eternal kingdom of God, but Jesus washes away that condemned sin for anyone who would put their full trust in Him. He ascends to the Father to prepare an eternal home for us. He sends the Spirit to abide in us as we abide in Him. This Holy Spirit is our down payment, seal, and guarantee for an eternal inheritance. And one day He will return to take us to be with Him forever: new heaven and new earth and holy city.

Every battle you fight...
Every decision you make...
Every challenge you face...
Every heartache you feel...
Every bill you pay...
Every love you share...

Every smile you form...
Every worry you submit to...

Everything fits into that eternal framework. The Bible never ignores or dismisses the reality of this life here on earth; it just redirects it from being primary to being secondary. The Bible is honest about the difficulties of this life; but it points to victory, not defeat. Jesus Himself said, "I have said these things to you, that in me you may have peace. In the world you will have tribulation. But take heart; I have overcome the world" (John 16:33). So, this perspective is not some "pie in the sky" or ignorant bliss. It is seeing reality—the way it was intended.

That is the purpose of this book: to give truth and examples and encouragement for seeing real life through eternal lenses. In essence, it is answering the question: *"How do I live out an eternal perspective in the real-life issues I am dealing with today?"*

This is my heart, transformed by the Word of God and the eternal gospel, put into writing. I hope you will journey with me by trying these glasses on for size.

SECTION 1:

"Though our outer self is wasting away..."

CHAPTER 1

2020

I F ASKED IN 2015 WHAT YOU WOULD BE DOING IN 5 years, you may have correctly predicted your occupation, grade level or family environment. But there is no way you would have predicted the events of 2020 and the impact they had on you and society. For that matter, you would have been inaccurate by January, just a month from everything breaking loose. Even if you could have predicted a worldwide pandemic, which many scientists have been warning about for years, you would not have coupled it with protests, injustices, political divisions, and so on. It was a year for the books, and I'm *not* referring to one of those feel-good stories.

It had all the makings for a banner year—or so we thought. Though some of us entered this new year considering it a great year to cast vision—20/20 vision—such a great analogy, but reality flipped that notion upside down. At this point, most of us would have settled for a normal, run-of-the-mill, ho-hum kind of year versus what we actually got.

Now admittedly, I have not lived through some of the most significant events and times of history. Throughout school, we learn of the founding of nations, wars that shaped culture, inventions that revolutionized life, and tragedies that shook folks out of their complacency.

I *have* experienced a few notable historical events in my lifetime. I remember being a freshman in high school when the space shuttle

Challenger exploded just over a minute after takeoff, killing all 7 astronauts on board. It consumed our day with shocking news coverage that played the event repeatedly. I remember September 11, 2001, I got to the office when news erupted of a plane flying into one of the towers of the World Trade Center. Then another. Then the Pentagon. We all wondered how many more there would be; how many places would be attacked? In both of those events, our nation came together, mourned together, and rose together.

I will also now be able to say that I lived through 2020. There is no doubt that 2020 will go down in history as one of the most tumultuous and difficult years in the common era. Rather than being a year of forward vision and optimism, 2020 turned into the year of simple survival. As a pastor and professor, I had non-stop decisions, conflict mitigations, and risk management.

We started the year with a virus that turned into a pandemic. This was not merely an American tragedy; it was worldwide. It spanned across ethnicities, cultures, and political systems. It brought death to the medically compromised and isolation to the masses. It divided us. There is still contention between the "masked" and the "unmasked." There are those who see nothing but government conspiracies, while others see the need for more government control. Every extreme imaginable is represented in our body of believers. It has been exhausting trying to keep the church united amid such divisiveness.

And if the 2020 pandemic was not enough for America, our country erupted in racial tensions as evidence of police brutality was caught on film and went viral. Rogue police officers were put on display as the norm for all law enforcement and unfairly tainting the overwhelming good done by those who had been considered "front line heroes" at the start of the COVID-19 lockdowns. Cities became war zones with protestors and rioters. Policies arose to defund the police. Terms like "social justice," "systemic racism," and "critical race theory" became divisive talking points with all sides using them for different agendas. "Black Lives Matter" faced off against "All Lives Matter" countered by the actual view of most people, "My Life and Opinion Matter Most."

Why stop there when we can throw in arguably the most heated and divisive political season in American history? It wasn't just the candidates—though they did their fair share of accusations, misrepresentations, and inciting discord. It was the public at large. The way people were treating each other during this election season made me nauseated, especially when it was people in the body of Christ. Social media gave an outlet to every individual to boldly proclaim their opinions and argue with—and insult—those who disagreed with them. It was sickening.

In all this turmoil of 2020, the church had a ripe opportunity to be on the forefront of pointing people to the gospel. It is, after all, in the darkest of nights that the light can shine the brightest. Yet, it seemed at times, that we were having to spend more energy on trying to keep the church united than being on mission in the fray of the world's despair. Whatever happened to humility, gentleness and unity? Whom do we actually serve: God, society, or self? Are we bound by the conventional wisdom of our culture or are we to rise above the junk, united under one Lord? Paul makes it clear:

> "I therefore, a prisoner for the Lord, urge you to walk in a manner worthy of the calling to which you have been called, with all humility and gentleness, with patience, bearing with one another in love, eager to maintain the unity of the Spirit in the bond of peace. There is one body and one Spirit—just as you were called to the one hope that belongs to your call—one Lord, one faith, one baptism, one God and Father of all, who is over all and through all and in all."
>
> –Ephesians 4:1-6

But there is a bright side, and this is where the eternal perspective comes in. If we don't have an eternal perspective, all the chaos and dysfunction around us is all we have. If our hope rests in mankind, then we are in massive trouble. The truth, however, is that the chaos and dysfunction all around us is *not* all we have. Our hope does *not* rest in mankind. It is imperative that we see the decay and difficulties of life through a new lens.

Here are some truths that will help us see clearly.

First, as I'm writing this, 2020 is about to end. Bring on 2021! That is a bit tongue in cheek. The fact is that the changing of the year means nothing if we don't change. Otherwise, we will take that same selfishness, arrogance, fear, and division into the new year. It will be a new year with new circumstances, but the same people. However, *we* can change. The more we conform to the Word and the Lord, the more we will make an eternal impact for the Kingdom of God.

Secondly, we should not be surprised when life gets worse here on earth. Now, I am not talking about a gloom and doom demeanor or a pessimistic attitude. In fact, it is because of an eternal perspective that we can acknowledge the grave outlook of man's situation and still have joy. Recognizing man's desperation and inabilities highlights the need for a Savior and the beauty of grace. This world has been stained by sin since the whole fruit incident in the garden. When Jesus came, He brought salvation and forgiveness of sin, conquering the effects of the grave. But until He comes again, this world is going to continue to slide into ungodliness and condemnation. We stand as lighthouses in this stormy darkness calling people to safety, hope, and peace.

Thirdly, we can be filled with gratitude for a Kingdom that cannot be shaken. Look at what it says in Hebrews 12:25-29:

> *See that you do not refuse him who is speaking. For if they did not escape when they refused him who warned them on earth, much less will we escape if we reject him who*

warns from heaven. At that time his voice shook the earth, but now he has promised, "Yet once more I will shake not only the earth but also the heavens." This phrase, "Yet once more," indicates the removal of things that are shaken— that is, things that have been made—in order that the things that cannot be shaken may remain. Therefore let us be grateful for receiving a kingdom that cannot be shaken, and thus let us offer to God acceptable worship, with reverence and awe, for our God is a consuming fire.

God is shaking things up. Those things that can be shaken will be removed. Those things that cannot be shaken will remain. If we are part of the shaken things, then either we do not belong to Him or we have taken our eyes off Him. Know this: we serve a God and live for a Kingdom that cannot be shaken and will remain. If we remain in Him, then we will not be shaken either, no matter how much this world rips apart.

Considering that truth, what should we do? *Be grateful!* As undeserving as we are, by His grace through faith we inherit the kingdom.

What else should we do? *Worship this all-consuming God in reverence and in awe.* It is only when we come to grips with who He truly is that we can embrace a full relationship with Him. He is not to be trifled with nor treated lightly. We are His friends because He called us friends, not because we are His equals.

One thing this difficult year has done is pruned the church. It has revealed motivations. It has spotlighted those who are in it for themselves and those who are in it for the mission of God's Kingdom. This pruning has been painful but necessary. The work ahead is not for the faint at heart or those with a consumer mentality. We don't have time to play casual faith games. Throughout the world, there are believers who have been on the frontlines in areas hostile to the gospel. Comfort and complacency have never been options for them. Now, it seems our society is heading in a direction where living out our faith may incur sacrifice. It might actually cost us something: time, reputation, money, health, etc. This is where true faith shines—on the frontlines.

An eternal perspective is not dismissive of the human condition but sees clearly and knows this is not all there is. We live in this kingdom as citizens of the coming Kingdom. Are you ready to live it out? *"For the kingdom of God does not consist in talk but in power"* (1 Corinthians 4:20).

CHAPTER 2

BROKEN

THE BOARD. A SIMPLE NOUN, BUT WHEN SPOKEN in the right context, it would immediately elevate my adrenaline. When I write "board," I'm not talking about a group of individuals who hold the power within an organization. I'm not referring to building materials found at your local Home Depot or Lowe's.

No, this board was different. This was where it all came down on Wednesday practices on game week of football at Riverview High School. During that mid-week practice, each non-starting player was given the chance to challenge the "first-stringer" above him on the board. If he beat the starter then he got to start in his place. It was basically two players, starting at opposite ends of a 2x4 that was about 6 feet long, ramming each other until one player was pushed backward past the end of the board. You get pushed off the board, you lose.

On a hot early October Wednesday, my time had come.

But let me set the stage for you.

The year was 1985. The worst year of my life. I had grown up in Winston-Salem, NC. For 16 years, my life had been anchored in that town. I was extremely active in my church and youth group. I was fully invested at my high school, moving up in student government and football. I had just gotten my driver's license and was beginning to experience the beginnings of a freedom I had never known. Life was

9

more than good. I was soaring. This was my life. Then, my world got shattered. I got the word that my family was getting ready to move to Sarasota, FL. *Are you kidding me?* I was finishing my sophomore year of high school. What a horrible time for a transition!

But there was nothing I could do about it.

I remember being emotionally distraught as we made our way down to the sunny Gulf Coast of Florida. One of the first things I did in the transition was join the varsity football team at Riverview High School and begin summer training and practices. Man, it was brutal! We practiced twice a day–in the "cool" of the morning and the "breeze" of the evening. The temps were crazy. However, what made it even more difficult was a completely different system than I was used to. As an offensive lineman, I had to learn new terminology and a whole new system of plays and blocking assignments. Having spent the first two years of my high school career in a different system put me at a disadvantage. I was way behind, and it showed.

Every week in practice, I gave it all I had. Every game, I watched 90% of it from the sideline. That's just the way it was. Every week, I challenged the starter above me. Every week, I realized that I should have started lifting weights earlier in my life! Every week, the starter crushed me.

Then came that fateful Wednesday in October.

"Alright, who wants the board?" said the line coach.

"I do!" I said, with forced enthusiasm. Part of me was shrugging. What's the point? The other part of me, that part that always tries optimistically to see the potential, was pumped up. I thought, *this could be my time. I'm going to give it all I've got.*

So, I jumped up there and strapped my helmet on. My opponent—my teammate—made his way to the board. I bent my knees, leaned forward stretching out my left arm and placed my hand on the ground. My right elbow barely touched my right leg. My right hand was balled into a fist. Sweat was dripping into my eyes. I shifted forward onto the balls of my feet and awaited the whistle.

It blew. I thrust my body forward into an incredible clash of shoulder pads, helmets, and flesh. I stayed low. I drove my powerful legs. We were caught in a stalemate in the middle of the board but then I felt him give a little. I took advantage and churned my legs. I got him off balance and eventually moved him past the board's edge. Yes! Round 1 goes to Coleman! Yes, round 1. You see, the board was best 2 out of 3.

Round 2: Same scenario...different ending. No stalemate on this one. He almost flipped me backward. I was exhausted. I didn't feel like I had anything left. But one round remained. I had no choice.

Round 3: I breathed deep, sucking in all the oxygen my heaving lungs could handle. I assumed my stance as my enemy and comrade faced off against me. We awaited the whistle, bodies pulsing, muscles tensed, adrenaline pumping, eyes locked on one another. Eyes that spoke volumes...eyes that said, "I don't hate you, but I'm getting ready to rip you apart, you're going down!"

The shrill of the whistle...
The clash of the warriors...
The legs digging...
The arms pushing, grabbing, slapping...
The muscles bulging...

And then it happened. I don't know exactly how it happened, but I felt my body going forward and his going backward. With every ounce of power and energy I had left in my failing flesh I surge forward. To the ground. I was on top of him. I shifted my head to the side and saw his end of the board. I had done it!! Some guys were shouting, others were cursing! They pulled me up. High fives all around. I could barely stand up. I was so exhausted. I reached out to shake my opponent's hand, but he refused. He had been "humiliated" by this newbie trans-plant from North Carolina.

But it was what it was; I was going to start my first varsity football game!

Friday night lights, here we go! It was time to suit up. Then I got hit on my blind side. "Coleman, you're not starting." A simple statement with no explanation, no animosity, no joy, no smirk...just a statement. But with that statement, I felt like I had been dropped off the top of the building.

> All the transitions in my life:
>   trying my best to make the most of it,
>   practicing every day,
>   barreling through every drill,
>   lifting every weight,
>   making every hit,
>   enduring every bruise on my multi-colored arms,
>   every yell from a coach...

Then the rug was pulled out from under me. I was devastated. I had been lied to, given false assurances, treated unfairly, abused...

My spirit was deflated—broken.

You most likely have not experienced the same board that I did, but you have no doubt had your own boards. The struggles of life that you have faced with either optimism or negativity, perseverance or for-feiting, power or weakness. The list could go on. There were times when you mustered everything you had and came out on top. There are other times when you gave up because you could not see the point in trying. Then there were times, like my board, when you persevered only to have the rug drug out from under you—the brutality of the results failing to live up to the effort exerted.

Struggles, tribulations, troubles, trials, sufferings—it really doesn't matter what you call them, they are common to all human beings. The Bible does not gloss over these difficulties. In fact, it displays them front and center; take a look at the cross of Christ for goodness sake. Coupled with the brutal honesty of life's struggles, God's Word gives us a consistent theme of victory.

Note the words of Jesus:

> *"I have said these things to you, that in me you may have peace. In the world you will have tribulation. But take heart; I have overcome the world."*–John 16:33

Cling to the promises of Jesus, right? Well, when Jesus promises that we will have trouble in this world, we often wish He would take that one back. Why does life have to be difficult? However, that promise is countered by another: "I have overcome this world!" He has not promised a life of comfort, ease, wealth, or health. But He has promised us victory. The knowledge that the world is ultimately under His sovereignty is a source of peace to us amid the trials.

This peace was not some simple, philosophical statement, naive wish, or the whimsical two-finger stickers. This was His life. During the most grueling persecution on the cross, He persevered. He managed to pray on behalf of others, promised salvation to a criminal, and made sure His mom would be cared for in His absence. How does one do that while dying on a cross? It comes from an eternal perspective.

Note the words of Paul in the central passage for this book:

> *"So we do not lose heart."* –2 Corinthians 4:16

These words echo verse 1 of chapter four. It means we do not faint, shrink back, or give up. In verse 1, we do not give up because we have received "this ministry by the mercy of God." What ministry is that?

It is the one we find immediately preceding this verse in 2 Corinthians 3:18: *"And we all, with unveiled face, beholding the glory of the Lord, are being transformed into the same image from one degree of glory to another. For this comes from the Lord who is the Spirit."* By faith, we understand that the path of life we are on is the journey by which God is transforming us. Basically, the Spirit is at work in us, not despite the circumstances we encounter, but *through* the circumstances we encounter.

In chapter 4, Paul talks about the hardships we face. These hardships are not reasons to hang our heads and give up the fight; rather, they are the platform by which we realize true victory. The victory being referred to is the glory of God in 2 Corinthians 4:15.

If this world is all there is, then losing heart would make a lot of sense. If my glory is a priority, then when I lose there is no reason to continue. If all that I am is all I'm ever going to be, then what is the point?

But Paul's and Jesus' point is that those perceptions are flat out wrong. This world is not all there is. In the same way the ditch in your front yard can't even be compared to the Grand Canyon, so this world cannot even compare to what is being prepared for us.

My days of playing competitive football are long gone, but my days of fighting on the board are not. The boards have changed shapes and sizes, but they still must be conquered. Sometimes, I wish it were as simple as going head-to-head with someone on the physical level. Often though, the boards come in financial difficulties, relationship struggles, job issues, car troubles, temptations, or tragedies! Any way you cut it, life is not easy.

But thankfully, we don't have to give up or lose hope. We know eventually, when this journey rounds the corner to the finish line, that we will be in victory lane. And there is no earthly coach who can sit you out of the starting lineup.

CHAPTER 3

JARS OF CLAY

T HE CITY CARRIED THE SAME SENSORY PERCEPTIONS of the other cities I had been to in China. There were masses of humanity everywhere and distinctive smells penetrated my nose. The din of horns blowing and people gabbing on cellphones pierced my ears. My eyes caught the awkward stares of the nationals as they tried to capture an overweight Caucasian westerner in their memories. The city was called Xi'an, located in the middle of China. Dr. Wilson and I had been training pastors for a week in the underground Christian church in another large city. After the training, we decided to take a train across the country to visit the Great Wall and Xi'an.

When we left Xi'an and ventured into the countryside, we had a mind-blowing experience. We encountered a massive army. We literally stood face to face with over 6,000 soldiers. An intimidating force equipped with horse mounted calvary, archers, and infantry. They were all poised in fighting position, daring us to make an aggressive move.

Of course, they lacked one vital element: breath of life.

Back in 1970, some Chinese farmers came across an incredible discovery in their farmland. One day, as they were working the ground for their crops, they came across a buried warrior made of clay. It belonged to the ancient mausoleum of Qin Shi Huang, the first emperor of China. The government was soon called in, confiscated the land, and the 45+ years of excavation work began that is still going on to this day. So far, they have unearthed over 6000 warriors. According to history, the king commissioned workers (i.e. slaves) to create for him an army to escort and guard him into the afterlife.

The whole exhibition was amazing. Each one of those soldiers has a distinctive look, from facial expressions and posture to adornments on their armor. I cannot fathom the amount of work this process took: carving every soldier with intricate detail, transporting them to the kiln, and then painting each one. Even the soles of the archers' shoes were carefully marked with circular tread. I am also amazed at the work it has taken to unearth these pieces—one by one. They are not even 1/4 of the way done after almost five decades of excavation!

There is one unmistakable takeaway from this exhibit: the "soldiers" did not achieve their purpose. The Chinese emperor is long dead and gone. His "terra cotta army" obviously did not make the journey into the afterlife with him. To the contrary, their bodies are still lifeless and broken in an underground museum while the archaeologists are painstakingly putting together the soldiers piece by piece. Thousands of years after they were created, they are still there.

As I reflected on this exhibit, I was reminded of what Paul told the Christians in Corinth: "But we have this treasure in jars of clay, to show that the surpassing power belongs to God and not to us" (2 Corinthians 4:7). What is this "treasure?" According to verse 6, this treasure is the "light of the knowledge of the glory of God in the face of Jesus Christ." The light has broken through the darkness of our souls. It has magnified the glory of God. It has changed everything in us. Yet, this special glorious treasure is transported in us, and he refers to us as "jars of clay."

Consider how we store and protect the things which we value: fire-proof safes, lock boxes, and vaults. We protect our investments. God has placed His incredible treasure in us—vessels that are fragile and weak! *Why?* Simple: the treasure is not only provided by Him as a gift, but also held by Him as a guarantee. It is His power, not ours, that keeps the treasure. He wants us to know that we are not only unworthy to have it, but we are also incapable of securing it. The only security that can hold such a treasure is His surpassing power.

It is not the nature of the container that gives value to the treasure. It is the nature of the treasure that transforms the nature of the container. That is why we can be

"afflicted, but not crushed

perplexed, but not driven to despair

persecuted, but not forsaken

struck down, but not destroyed." –2 Corinthians 4:8-9

Every minute we live in these earthly bodies, we are dying. These bodies, corrupted by a sin nature do not stand a chance in this world. Ashes to ashes and dust to dust, these bodies will waste away. The terra cotta warriors are no worse off than the destiny of our fleshly bodies.

However, our temporary bodies hold the Light of the world.

Paul goes on to state, "Always carrying in the body the death of Jesus, so that the life of Jesus may also be manifested in our bodies. For we who live are always being given over to death for Jesus' sake, so that the life of Jesus also may be manifested in our mortal flesh" (vv.10-11). His glory is manifested in our simple, fragile bodies. If we were magnificent pieces of art, vases of pristine crystal, diamond-laden sculptures, or platinum trophies, then maybe we would run the risk of attempting to steal some of His glory. However, we are jars of clay and there is nothing significant about us. Our significance is not in who we are but what we carry.

The beauty is that these jars of clay will one day inherit bodies that are indestructible. These bodies, or tents as Paul later calls them, are groaning for something greater...our heavenly dwelling. You and I were built for eternity.

"For we know that if the tent that is our earthly home is destroyed, we have a building from God, a house not made with hands, eternal in the heavens. For in this tent we groan, longing put on our heavenly dwelling, if indeed by putting it on we may not be found naked. For while we are still in this meant we groan, being burdened—not that we would be unclothed, but that we would be further clothed, so that what is mortal may be swallowed up by life. He who has prepared us for this very thing is God, who has given us the Spirit as a guarantee."

–2 Corinthians 5:1-5

Your body becomes a victim and vessel of your sinful nature and, therefore, cannot inherit heaven. But never fear, you have an eternal body crafted by the very hands of God awaiting you. As believers, we need not fear entering eternity naked. He will clothe us with an indestructible body. He gave His Spirit to guarantee just that.

Paul further displays the striking differences between our earthly bodies and the ones we will inherit. Soak in the distinctives of the different bodies.

"So is it with the resurrection of the dead.
What is sown is **perishable**; what is raised is **imperishable**.
It is sown in **dishonor**; it is raised in **glory**.
It is sown in **weakness**; it is raised in **power**.
It is sown a **natural body**; it is raised a **spiritual body**.
If there is a natural body, there is also a spiritual body."

These bodies we possess right now will not last, but the ones to come will never waste away. These skins we wear are constantly either battling or embracing the impact of the inherited sin nature. However, the ones to come will be in complete compliance with the glory of God. These shells are weak, while the coming bodies are powerful. These tents are weighed down by the laws and instincts of the natural. The ones we will put on will be supernaturally freed from those constraints.

So, yeah, we acknowledge the fight against death, COVID-19, cancer, diabetes, AIDS, paralysis, dementia, and thousands of other ailments. We admit that there is a struggle against addiction, lust, immorality, cheating, pride, greed, and thousands of other sins.

However, we embrace the truth that this is not all there is. There is a glorified body that awaits believers in Jesus Christ that will make all these temporary concerns pale in comparison.

So, lift up that heavy head. Pull back those wearied shoulders. Stand that sore back up to attention. For in that jar of clay that you call an earthly body, that seems to be weak and frail and worn out lies the Treasure of the universe which guarantees it will all be worth it one day.

CHAPTER 4

STOP BLOCKING THE LIGHT

AN AMAZON MISSION TRIP IS NOT FOR THE FAINT of heart. For a week-long mission trip, we rode in a double-decker, open-air boat from which swung 35 or so hammocks. These suspended beds were no farther than a short arm's length away from each other. Some were situated so close that a dictionary would not fit between them. Hammocks are wonderful for relaxing, but they are not the easiest to sleep in when you are not used to it. These conditions were not for the those who value comfort or the more claustrophobic among us.

The days were hot; the evenings were hot. The water was about the only thing that was cool. And since the shower on our boat was pumping up that Amazon River water, it was cool and refreshing. But as soon as we finished our showers, we started sweating again before we could get our clothes on. Even the nights were hot—even hotter when you factor in a zipped-up bug net since the boat was tied to a tree with a few hornets' nests who were mixing it up with the mosquitos! We honestly had to lower our expectations for comfort, embrace 24/7 sweating, and fix our eyes on the purpose for the mission. When we did, some amazing moments flooded our experience. These came primarily in relationships and seeing lives impacted by the hands and feet and the gospel of the Savior. But they also came in the realm of nature.

At night, in more remote parts of the Amazon River, there are few lights, if any, emitting a glow from the shoreline. Our only lights came from the boat. But something amazing happened when they turned off those lights. As our eyes adjusted to the darkness, a spectacle of brilliance went on display that cannot be rivaled by anything man has created. I have never seen so many stars in my life! I never saw so many constellations or saw the Milky Way so clearly. We were a long way from city life. Back home we get a simple appetizer of the star buffet. On the dark Amazon, the sky comes alive. It is breathtaking. Mesmerizing.

Then, when we had the opportunity, we sat on the front of the boat and caught a glimpse of the reflection of that celestial master-piece in the water below. With billions of stars above and the same amount being mirrored below, it is a fascinating spectacle. It was as if we were suspended in space and sitting at the edge of the galaxy. In those moments, with nearly 40 people on the boat, everyone sat in breathless wonder. Some things are just too awe-inspiring to mess up with words.

When the lights of the boat came back on, something equally astonishing, but simultaneously discouraging happened—the stars disappeared. We could see a handful of stars here and a constellation there, but 99% of them "vanished."

It's like those spy glasses that came with those books when I was a kid. Without the glasses, the page would just look like a palette of colors. When you put the glasses on a secret message appeared. The message was always there, but you couldn't see it without the perspective of the glasses. The stars are always there, but the competing light, in closer proximity, drowns out their beauty.

And then the bugs came. Buzzing, nagging, irritating bugs. They were attracted to the artificial light of the boat.

Our lives are barraged daily by competing light. These are the lights that are birthed out of the temporary which demand our attention due to their proximity and brightness. They urgently call for our devotion and allegiance.

But alas, they are frauds. Their promise of satisfaction is a hoax. These are the lights that lure us to trade the eternal for the temporary, beg us to sin, and create worry, pain, and discontent. These are the lights that not only block out the beauty of the eternal, but they also bring the pests of life out into the open. You know the kind: the ones who stir up drama, or who seek to use us for their own benefit. Everything is an emergency; everything is critical. They dine on the trivial and feast on drama.

The truth is that these imposter lights are really birthed out of darkness. The Bible is full of talk about spiritual light and darkness. The apostle John consistently highlighted the contrast between light and darkness. In fact, he even started his gospel by putting it on the forefront in John 1:4-5, 9:

> "In him [Jesus] was life, and the life was the light of men. The light shines in the darkness, and the darkness has not overcome it.... The true light, which gives light to everyone, was coming into the world."

Note how John refers to Jesus in John 1:9: the true light. He is the one true light. Forget the false, wannabe lights which are mere flickers of temporal matchsticks. Jesus is the one, true Light. John walked by His side and knew it was true.

It makes complete sense that John raised a theological eyebrow and chose to record what Jesus said about Himself as the light of the world. Take a look:

> "I am the light of the world. Whoever follows me will not walk in darkness, but will have the light of life."
> –John 8:12

"As long as I am in the world, I am the light of the world." –John 9:5

He makes the claim here to be the light of the world. Now, this is an incredible self-assertion by Jesus, but it takes on even more significance when seen in the context of which it was spoken.

Jesus said "I am light of the world" near the conclusion of the Festival of Tabernacles (or Booths). This was the annual feast that drew Jews into a time of remembrance for God's provision for them during their wandering in the wilderness following the exile from slavery in Egypt. During this time, the Jews would make for themselves makeshift booths or tents to live in during the week-long festival. These booths represented their living arrangements in the wilderness.

Light played an important role in the festival because the pillar of fire led the Israelites by night in the wilderness. Check out this description:

> Four huge menorahs were set up to illuminate the entire Temple area. In actuality they were so large that each of the stems formed a torch. The wicks were made from the worn out linen garments of the priests. As smaller torches were carried to light the procession, the people danced and played harps, lyres, cymbals and lutes. The Levites chanted the Psalms of Ascent (120-134); one psalm on each of the fifteen steps leading from the court of the Israelites to the court of the women. Imagine what a glorious scene it must have been, with the majesty of the procession and the golden stone walls of the Temple bathed in the glow of the torch-lit night![1]

---

[1] "Sukkot: A Promise of Living Water," Jews for Jesus, accessed June 6, 2019, https://jews-forjesus.org/publications/issues/issues-v06-n07/sukkot-a-promise-of-living-water/.

Incredible! As the temple stood elevated on the temple mount in Jerusalem, it no doubt could be seen from all over the city and beyond. It is in this context that Jesus makes this powerful proclamation. He is not simply the light of Jerusalem or the light of the Judean region. Even the whole of Israel was too small to contain this light. No. Jesus is the *Light of the world*. He is the only true Light for all the Middle East, Africa, Asia, the Americas and the entire world population. He is the only true Light for every religion as well. In the midst of all world religions with their various leaders and scriptures, only One stands above the rest. That kind of exclusive statement seems pretty offensive given the pluralistic leanings of our society. Regardless of offense, though, it is what Jesus said and it is truth.

So, the true Light was there, is here, and will remain. It is an eternal Light after all. Our inability to see this Light is not because He is insufficient or has left us alone. It is because we have allowed the smaller, insignificant lights to blind us from the truth.

We desperately need to stop letting the "little lights" dominate our perspective. We must stop letting the things of this world distort our vision of the eternal. It simply takes flipping the temporal light switch off, to once again see the eternal glory of it all.

CHAPTER 5

WHERE IS THE HOPE?

"**H**OW CAN WE PRAY FOR YOU?" I ASKED HER. "You can pray that I will go ahead and die quickly."

Her words stung me.

This lady in her 80's stood in the doorway of her run-down stucco house. She was hunched over and struggling to walk. She was dressed in traditional clothing for older Moldovan women living in a village: skirt, shawl, and a scarf around her head.

Let me share the context surrounding this interaction. I had taken a team to Moldova. We were working in an obscure village that you would have trouble finding on Google Earth without using the search icon. Part of our team was doing construction on a building recently acquired by a small church, and the other part of the team was doing a medical clinic. There were a few team members who were with me and a translator taking bags of food to elderly residents. We were maneuvering through these heavily worn dirt roads. The ruts on these roads would make you laugh at what we call potholes back in the States.

These residents could easily be classified as elderly orphans. Work is so scarce in these areas that when folks reach a working age, they typically leave the village to go find work. Sometimes they even leave the country. They leave behind their aging parents and grandparents with promises to send back resources. Sometimes that happens, sometimes it does not. These precious souls are often forgotten and desperate. They don't need smart phones and calendar apps; their primary task is to make it another day.

Into this setting, we joined with a local church and brought bags full of rice, beans, canned meat, pasta, butter, oil, barley, and more. We would knock on doors and hand them these bags. We use the provision of daily bread as a bridge to talk about the Bread of life. We held their dirty, wrinkled, chapped hands. We offered to pray for them. Sometimes we would sing. Sometimes we would fetch water. But at all times, we showed them attention and love.

There are so many powerful stories that we have encountered through doing this one simple specific mission task. This lady was one of those stories.

We walked into her dirt yard and past her starving dog who was chained up. We knocked on the door and waited. And waited. We knocked several times. Our translator was convinced that she was there. I was doubting it. We began to leave when the door opened very slowly, and a well-worn elderly lady appeared. She was hanging on to the doorframe as if it were all she had to hold her up. Veins rose from her aged hands like rivers running through a desert. The scarf wrapped around her head was knotted under her chin. Her face revealed her age and much more. Life had not been easy, or even fair. As far as we could see inside the doorway, her home was dirty, dark and hopeless.

We introduced ourselves. Americans in a village like this one, approaching a house like this one, to speak to a woman like this one... well, that just does not happen often. We handed her the bag of food and witnessed the briefest moment of joy come across those eyes. She quickly put the bag down as the weight of it could have almost toppled her over.

We told her that we had come from America to let her know that Jesus loved her and had not forgotten her. He offered her hope and salvation. She then told us, "It is too late for me."

Before I share further about this conversation, just to be clear, a little more cultural context would be helpful. This woman is most likely of the Orthodox faith, as are over 95% of Moldovans. The Orthodox faith, though still believing in Jesus, places a high value on rituals (kissing icons, lighting candles, etc.) and good works. Concepts like forgiveness and grace, core principles of the biblical gospel, are not emphasized. Assurance of salvation is very hard to hold onto because so much is based upon the individual's faithfulness to the rituals. It is based more on the performance of the person rather than the action and gift of our God.

When we go to countries like Moldova on mission trips, our ultimate goal is not to sway people from their traditional religious upbringing as much as it is to introduce them to the pure gospel of Jesus Christ. What He did for us can accomplish for us what we could never do on our own. No matter what we do, we will never be able to earn the grace of God. No matter what we do, we will never be too far from the reach of the grace of God.

Most villages in Moldova have an Orthodox Church which is run by a priest. In general, the priests have great influence in the village communities. Typically, with a bit of paranoid disdain, they proclaim that evangelical churches are cults and should be avoided by their Orthodox church members. Thus, church planting in these areas is very difficult. We endeavor to partner with these church plants and ministries that are working to shine the light of Christ in dark places.

So, back to our story: think for a minute about this woman's perspective. If she has lived her whole life under the religious belief that you have to work to make God happy, then it begins to make sense that she would say it is too late for her. She is now old. She can barely leave or even maneuver through her house. She can't make it to the Orthodox church, light the proper candles or kiss the proper icons. She is homebound with nothing to offer anyone, especially God.

Her statements are consistent with her broken theology:

"It is too late for me."

"Pray that God lets me die quickly."

But the theology of this precious woman is wrong.

It is not too late. As long as there is breath in our lungs, there is hope. The offer of grace is not dependent upon age. It is not dictated by what you, me, or this lady can bring to the table or do in our own strength. It is driven by the love of God.

I tried to share this with her, that we had been sent from America to communicate the truth of God's incomprehensible love, that He was not oblivious nor insensitive to her plight. The fruit of a relationship with the Creator, born out of the cross and resurrection, could be experienced by her that very day.

This truth contrasts her second statement as well. Her life was tough, and she was presumably on her own. In her mind, the best thing to do would be to go ahead and die...quickly. What's the point of continuing to live when things are this bad? I heard the struggle and despair in her voice. She was weary and ready to throw in the towel.

But the voice of the Lord is stronger. All hope is not lost—even in the midst of despair.

Under arrest for proclaiming the gospel, Paul stated,

> *"For to me to live is Christ, and to die is gain. If I am to live in the flesh, that means fruitful labor for me. Yet which I shall choose I cannot tell. I am hard pressed between the two. My desire is to depart and be with Christ, for that is far better. But to remain in the flesh is more necessary on your account."*
>
> –Philippians 1:21-24

Paul was struggling, too. Paul actually saw benefit in dying, not so much to leave this difficult world but to embrace the one to come. Nevertheless, the timing was God's call to make, not Paul's. As long as Paul was alive, he would live for Jesus, embracing the gospel mission. When the time came to die, it would only get better.

I so wanted this sweet lady to gain that supernatural perspective. I desired for her eyes to be open to grace and love and hope. I longed to see her spend her last days on this earth consumed with peace and joy, regardless of the physical limitations of a body that was failing. However, 8 decades of being told that the weight of salvation all depended on her was too much for her to shake off. She just wanted to die because she was convinced it was too late for her.

We reached out and held her hands and prayed. She cried. We cried. And we continue to pray that the Holy Spirit planted a seed in her heart that day that took root with the truth: You are never too old...never unloved...never too far gone...never without hope.

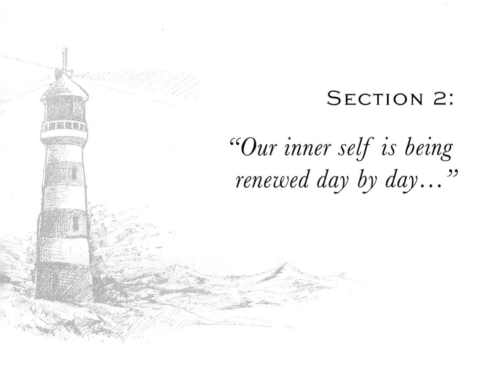

SECTION 2:

"Our inner self is being renewed day by day..."

CHAPTER 6

THIS I KNOW

"IWOULD REALLY LIKE TO SIT DOWN AND TALK with you sometime." These were the words that led a meeting at a local coffee shop with Margaret, me, and my wife.

After a few minutes of small talk, I broke the silence with, "So, what's up?" Cue the tears and shaking head. I asked her to start from the beginning.

Church background. Alcoholic and abusive father. Started drinking at 16. Life of mistakes. Attended AA, got Sober. Fell back into the drink. She was ashamed and humiliated.

As we talked, it became clear that though she had tasted bitter religion, she had never tasted the sweet nectar of a relationship with Christ. I shared the gospel and asked her if she wanted to trust Jesus and enter into a relationship with Him. She said, "Yes, but that is something for people who are better than me."

I said, smiling, "Margaret, have you heard anything I have said? He loves you. He knows everything about you. And He *still* loves you. You, with all of your flaws and mistakes and failures and relapses, are exactly why He left His throne to come down to a cross. I know He loves you. You are tired of failing—of being miserable. You have tried as hard as you can, but nothing has worked. And now you are hesitant to put your faith in Him because you fear you'll fail at being a Christian too.

But that is not how it works. Something supernatural happens when you put your faith in Jesus. He changes everything. You can't "better" yourself. He is the one who changes you, but you have to surrender your control and give Him everything you got—this is what faith in Christ looks like."

What about you? Do you really believe that? His grace is available: His grace is sufficient. There is nothing you or I can do to override or diminish the power of God's grace.

And His grace flows out of His love for us. If you have had any contact with the church in your past, or even if you have watched a football game on TV, you have seen or heard a reference to John 3:16. This beloved verse is so well known that it can get recited without a second thought. Read it again for the first time:

For God
so loved
the world
that He gave
His only begotten Son
that whosoever
believes
in Him
should not perish
but have everlasting life.

Each of those lines is a sermon in itself.

Each of those lines is enhanced by other Scriptures.

Each of those lines displays of the heart of the Creator of the Universe.

Each of those lines is a call to turn from eternal death.

Each of those lines is a call to embrace eternal life.

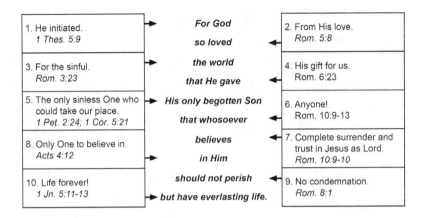

I'm reminded of an incredible story we find in Luke 7. A Pharisee had invited Jesus over for dinner. While they are eating, a "woman of the city" (v. 37) comes into the house when she heard that Jesus was there. Her specific sins are not detailed, but her status as a known sinner is made clear (vv. 37, 39, 47). No doubt all eyes were on her as she entered that house. I can hear the rumblings as I read this story. "What is *she* doing here?" "Good grief, does Simon know this sinner has come in here?" "Somebody needs to get the riffraff out of here."

But the lady keeps moving. Like a baseball pitcher who blocks out the deafening noise of the crowd to focus in on the catcher's signal for the perfect pitch, she zeroes in on Jesus. The haughty judgmental stares become a blur. The caustic, hurtful words being lobbed at her become white noise in her ears. The closer she gets, the more the tears fall, splashing on the soiled feet of the Savior. She begins to wipe them from his feet with her hair. But that is not enough for the only One who could love her so purely. She began to kiss those unwashed feet. But even that would not suffice. She took the perfumed oil that she had brought with her for a purpose and bathed his feet with the expensive ointment.

Such a reckless expression of unabashed love, gratitude and humility must have made the attenders very uncomfortable. In fact, Simon the Pharisee took this as a sure sign that Jesus was not a prophet. If Jesus were from God, He surely would have known how horrible a sinner this woman was (v.39). After all, one can imagine what unrighteous acts she engaged in to afford such an expensive item. However, if Jesus were not from God, how would He be able to read Simon's thoughts? And amazingly, that is exactly what happened. Jesus *answered* Simon's thoughts!

Jesus gives the Pharisee a scenario whereby two debtors are forgiven. One owed a year and a half of wages and the other about a month and a half. Which one would be the most grateful? Simon had to admit that it would be the one whom carried the largest debt.

Then Jesus makes a remarkable comparison. He tells Simon that this sinful woman, in her gratitude and love, had shown Him more hospitality than His host. Whereas Simon had not provided a simple courtesy of water to wash His dusty, dirty feet, the woman provided her tears. Whereas this Pharisee had not greeted Jesus with a customary welcome kiss on the cheek, this sinner kissed the feet of Jesus. Whereas this host had not anointed Jesus' head with oil, this outsider anointed his feet with the ointment.

In her sin, this woman found the forgiveness of a Savior and it blew her away. It transformed her and she could never be the same. Nothing she had was too good to lay at the feet of Jesus. Getting her hair dirty? No problem. Pressing her lips against His feet? No worries. Spilling out expensive perfume? No thought about it.

I love the way my friend William Wilson phrased it. "Her actions reveal the cry of her heart. This is what she has found: that Jesus is better. He's better than sin. One look at His face and she's lost a taste for it. Jesus is worthy of her perfume. He is better than an expensive thing."[2]

---

[2] William Wilson. "Jesus is Everything." A sermon preached at He's Alive Church on September 8, 2019. https://vimeo.com/358688218 Accessed September 11, 2019.

A sinner with nothing but heartache, regrets and shame bowed before the King. She believed in Jesus. He had forgiven her (v.48). She did not earn His forgiveness by her powerful display. No. Her powerful display of love was a response to a more powerful display of forgiveness. And now, she could go in peace (v.50).

This woman reminds me of our friend, Margaret. A tornado of heartache cannot bring down a house built on the foundation of the King's mercy. A tumultuous sea of regrets cannot sink a boat anchored to the Savior's grace. A hurricane of shame cannot destroy an island that is resting on the top of the Lord's love.

Margaret had to understand that starting a relationship journey with Christ had nothing to do with her performance. It had everything to do with responding to the gift being offered to her by the eternal Lover of her soul. She had never had such an offer from someone Who would never fail her, leave her, kick her to the curb, or let her go. Until now.

And she trusted Him that day in a local coffee shop. She bowed her head and gave everything up. And as she lifted her head, with tears streaming down her face, I gazed into the eyes of the redeemed. The object of His affection—one whom He valued enough to take her place on a cross of death.

And every bit of that moment was ultimately for His eternal glory. We were created for His glory. The cross was for His glory, so was our salvation, our surrender, abundant life, eternal life—all for His glory.

Margaret's life changed in that moment—for His glory.

Jesus loves me...this I know...for the Bible tells me so...

Chapter 7

Your Funeral

W OULD YOU RATHER ATTEND A BIRTHDAY PARTY
or a funeral? Seems like a crazy question, doesn't it?

Birthday parties are full of excitement.
Funerals are usually solemn.

Birthday parties celebrate life moving forward.
Funerals celebrate a life that has passed.

Birthday parties bring gifts.
Funerals bring flower arrangements.

Birthday parties bring smiles and joy.
Funerals bring tears and grief.

Funerals are not fun. Even the ones that aim for celebration still sting. Funerals remind us that someone we loved is no longer around. Funerals remind us of the brevity of life, that constitutes a moment in time, but the pain and grief of loss can linger for a lifetime. Even when life seems to be clipping along, news of death can hit us out of nowhere, paralyzing us.

I have an odd question that I want you to consider: Have you attended your own funeral yet? Wait...not so fast. Just hear me out and think this one through; *have you attended your own funeral yet?*

The question sounds preposterous because anyone who could actually answer it would be alive, right? Stick with me.

Physical life and death are fairly easy to discern. Are you breathing? Is your heart beating? Even so, with modern medicine and technology, the presence of life can get murky. Is life reduced to merely a heartbeat and functioning lungs or is there something else to it? Where does brain function, awareness, and consciousness fit into the equation? Anyone who has had to decide whether to "pull the plug" understands this modern-day dilemma.

The Bible does not neglect the physical aspect of life and death. Throughout its pages, we see babies born and people dying. Sometimes babies are born into positions of power like King Josiah, while other times those births happen in the most difficult of circumstances like with Moses and Jesus. Death can come naturally as it did for Abraham, or as a result of war as with Saul, or martyrdom as for Stephen, and still other times there is divine judgement like there was for Achan. We see these biblical examples and can make some direct correlations to our own physical understanding of death.

However, the Bible says a lot more about life and death than just limiting it to the physical view. In John 3, we see a religious leader in the Jewish community named Nicodemus coming to Jesus seeking truth. Jesus blew his mind when he told him that he had to be born again. Preposterous! How can a human re-enter a womb and be reborn? On a physical level, it makes no sense. However, Jesus explains that the flesh is one thing, but the spirit is another. Alive in the flesh means very little unless one has been made alive in the spirit.

All living humans have experienced physical birth. All living humans will experience physical death. *"And just as it is appointed for man to die once, and after that comes judgment, so Christ, having been offered once to bear the sins of many, will appear a second time, not to deal with sin but to save those who are eagerly waiting for him"* (Hebrews 9:27-28). Even if you live to see the second coming of Christ, your current body is not going to make it to heaven. *"I tell you this, brothers: flesh and blood cannot inherit the kingdom of God, nor does the perishable inherit the imperishable"* (1 Corinthians 15:50).

The Word goes on to explain that we must die to live. Paul states that he has been crucified with Christ and he no longer lives, but Christ lives in him (Galatians 2:20). Even though he was still alive in the flesh, he was raised to a new life of faith. In a sense, before the resurrection of our spirits, we are walking around spiritually dead.

I have never been a huge zombie fan in the entertainment world, but there are few movies/shows that have struck a chord with me. "I Am Legend" follows one man and his dog as they face life in a world where, to his knowledge, the only other humans left have turned into flesh eating zombies. A key theme in the movie is the desperation of isolation.

"The Walking Dead" is a popular TV series centered around a group of individuals navigating a world with masses of zombies and the ever-constant threat of other human clans competing for limited resources.

Truth be told, both works of entertainment are more about interpersonal relationships than cutting off the heads of the undead. Ironically, the term "walking dead" may refer more to the living than the dead.

Our spiritual condition before faith is very similar to zombies. We are driven by passions and instinct rather than truth. Self-preservation and self-satisfaction rise to the top of our priorities.

> *"And you were dead in the trespasses and sins in which you once walked, following the course of this world, following the prince of the power of the air, the spirit that is now at work in the sons of disobedience—among whom we all*

*once lived in the passions of our flesh, carrying out the
desires of the body and the mind, and were by nature
children of wrath, like the rest of mankind."*

–Ephesians 2:1-3

The zombies are consumed with hunger for human flesh. Nothing else matters. They don't distinguish between people. They don't evaluate morality or ethics. They eat and never get satisfied.

In our flesh, we are hungry for whatever satisfies self. Other people become tools and resources to achieve our goals. We have a built-in moral center, but compromise is inevitable as we pursue self-satisfaction. Even our most noble efforts can ultimately be birthed out of serving self: our desire to feel needed, valuable or appreciated.

When we die to the flesh, the satisfaction switches from self to God. The glory we seek is not our own, but His. We realize the foundation and nature of our fleshly desires and we yearn for those destructive desires to be transformed into the desires God has planned for us.

Now, when we are in our zombified, spiritual existence, there is no struggle or battle. Everything is embraced through the lens of self-satisfaction. When we are born again spiritually, we take on a dual nature and enter into the battle. We begin to have this flesh versus spirit conflict. We are being prompted to enter that arena, which is predicated upon us dying. Yes, we must die in order to fight. *This is not a fight to the death; rather, this is death to the fight.*

I must have my funeral before I can have my birthday party. Take a moment to walk through these verses and recognize the changing identity you and I have in Christ.

*"Those who belong to Christ Jesus have crucified the flesh
with its passions and desires."*

–Galatians 5:24

When Jesus was crucified on the cross, he took my sins upon His sinless body. I do not have to pay for my sins; however, by faith in Him, I crucify the passions and desires of the flesh.

> *"We know that our old self was crucified with him in order that the body of sin might be brought to nothing, so that we would no longer be enslaved to sin. For one who has died has been set free from sin. Now if we have died with Christ, we believe that we will also live with him. We know that Christ, being raised from the dead, will never die again; death no longer has dominion over him. For the death he died he died to sin, once for all, but the life he lives he lives to God. So you also consider yourselves dead to sin and alive to God in Christ Jesus."*
> –Romans 6:6-11

We die with Christ now we live with Christ. He was crucified and our old lives were crucified with Him. He rose from the dead, and we are raised to a new life.

> *"For as in Adam all die, so also in Christ shall all be made alive."*
> –1 Corinthians 15:22

We inherited sin and death through Adam. We inherited righteousness and life through Christ.

> *"Even when we were dead in our trespasses, made us alive together with Christ—by grace you have been saved."*
> –Ephesians 2:5

It is not simply that we were bad people who needed to become good. We were dead people who needed to come to life! By God's grace we received the life that we did not deserve.

> "Therefore, if anyone is in Christ, he is a new creation. The old has passed away; behold, the new has come."
>
> –2 Corinthians 5:17

We no longer live for the old ways. We have new life. We have replaced dialing numbers on a rotary dial phone to speed dialing on a smart phone. We speak into a GPS rather than figure out how to refold that old paper map. We have traded in Pong for the newest Xbox or PlayStation. I might as well quit dating myself—you get the point.

> "But far be it from me to boast except in the cross of our Lord Jesus Christ, by which the world has been crucified to me, and I to the world. For neither circumcision costs for anything, nor uncircumcision, but a new creation."
>
> –Galatians 6:14-15

It is no longer sufficient to follow rituals, rules or regulations to gain a standing before God. He is about transforming hearts, not transforming behavior. Don't misunderstand: a new heart most certainly leads to new behavior. However, changing behavior without changing the heart is hard, meaningless work.

One of my best friends is Mark Carnes. We have certainly gotten ourselves into some crazy things over the years; or more accurately: he has put me up to some crazy things! A few years ago, God opened the door and kicked him through to start a new church. After much prayer, it was decided that this new church would have a unique, but powerful name. They called it He's Alive Church.

This name was somewhat related to a practice Mark has of going out in the wee hours of the morning every Easter and yelling into a megaphone: "He's Alive!!" No doubt this has disturbed the sleeping bliss of many neighbors! "Jesus rose from the dead, now get yourself out of bed!"

The name, however, was more significant than a simple megaphone. The tagline or motto for He's Alive Church is "Bringing Life to Dead Places." I love this statement. The Bible clearly speaks of death and darkness. While it is easy to point out the death and darkness in our world around us, the first place to point is within us. We are full of death and darkness and need the life and light of the gospel of Jesus Christ to invade our deepest being. Thankfully, that invasion is exactly what takes place when we put our faith in Him. Death is defeated and replaced with His life. Sin is overcome by His righteousness. Darkness is conquered with His light.

By God's direction, calling, and grace, He led me to join Mark at He's Alive to lead His people forward in faith. Every transition in my ministry life reminds me of that day way back when I was 5 years old and was born again. Every step along the way was part of the journey of growing up in Christ until the day He takes me to be with Him.

So, your spiritual funeral ushers in your first true spiritual birthday. And it is a momentous occasion. I mean, even the angels in heaven get in on that party. *Just so, I tell you, there is joy before the angels of God over one sinner who repents* (Luke 15:10). Understanding the nature of true life in Christ is essential to maintaining an eternal perspective.

The funeral / first birthday party is just the beginning of the journey.

CHAPTER 8

THE PRESCRIPTION FOR PEACE

A N UNEXPECTED, UN-BUDGETED BILL COMES IN the mail demanding to be paid in 20 days.

Someone you considered a close friend betrays you.

Your son is a soldier stationed in another nation and you have not heard from him in weeks.

You walk into the NICU and see parents holding a newborn breathing only by a manual resuscitation pump and they say, "We wanted to keep him alive until you got here."

Your spouse walks out on you and into the arms of another lover.

When your 16-year-old goes out that first night driving by themselves severely warned that they better be home by 10pm.

Depression and fear continually knock at your mind's door distracting you from much needed sleep.

Your boss says she needs to talk to you with a grim look on her face.

The doctor says that you should hear the results of the tests in about a week.

Your parent has succumbed to the effects of dementia and does not even remember your name.

You drive away from the college campus realizing that everything you have invested in your kid must now withstand the pressure of the world without your daily influence.

Trust me. I'm not trying to be "Dougie Downer" here. But these situations are reality. All of these realities represent the conditions which can usher in turbulent storms in our souls.

Worry literally means to be pulled in two different directions. The Old English root for worry is "strangled." In Middle English, it literally meant "to grab by the throat and tear."[3] That is rather violent, but if you have suffered from worry, you know that description can be pretty accurate. Have you ever been strangled by worry? Where does worry or anxiety come from? It comes from the mind (wrong thinking) and from the heart (wrong feeling).

On the other end of the spectrum is peace and rest. It is contrasted with strife. It is a state of untroubled, undisturbed well-being. It is calmness of the soul. One may think that the best peace results from being in the ideal settings and circumstances. As peaceful as it might be to sit on the beach, toes in the ocean, sweet tunes in your earphones, book in hand, and drink by your side, this setting is still the not ideal peace. The best peace is when you can have a restful soul regardless of the circumstances that surround you.

Which would you rather have in your life: worry and strife or peace and rest?

Did you know that peace is actually promised in Scripture? It is a conditional promise, which means that something needs to happen to access this promise.

If you have a physical or mental ailment, you may have a prescription for medicine that will help with your symptoms. Cancer may require chemotherapy, radiation, or surgery. A common cold may require over the counter cold remedies. An infection needs an anti-biotic. Some medicines cure the malady, while others help to keep the symptoms at bay. You can't necessarily choose the medical

---

3   https://www.merriam-webster.com/dictionary/worry?src=search-dict-box
    Accessed September 12, 2019.

condition you have, but you can choose whether or not you take your meds.

In a similar way, you often have little choice on the circumstances you face in life, but God has offered us a prescription for internal peace regardless of what we face on the outside. God is not going to force His peace on you, but He freely offers it to those who want it.

So, what is the prescription for this peace in our lives?

While writing his letter to the church at Philippi, Paul finds himself under arrest. Amazingly, despite his circumstances, Paul pens this letter which has been often called the "Letter of Joy." How does one have joy while being under arrest for sharing truth? It is all about an eternal perspective. In Philippians 4:4-7, Paul gives us 4 commands that will bring about the promise of peace.

The first element of this prescription is to rejoice in verse 4. It may seem baffling to us that we are to rejoice when difficulties come our way. Paul knows that his readers may have trouble grasping this concept, so he repeats it for emphasis: "again I will say, rejoice." Our confusion at such a statement is birthed out of a flawed mentality that tells us our mental attitude is subservient to our outside influences. In other words, we are strapped into the roller coaster of life. The highs and lows of the tracks will determine our internal mental and emotional attitudes.

Rejoicing, however, is not limited to being a consequence of good things happening in our lives. It actually can be a catalyst for seeing life through a different lens. There are few things in life we can control but choosing to rejoice is fully within our control.

James gives a similar sentiment in James 1:2-5. "Count it all joy, my brothers, when you meet trials of various kinds, for you know that the testing of your faith produces steadfastness. And let steadfastness have its full effect, that you may be perfect and complete, lacking in nothing." Rather than let the waves of this world drown you, view them through the prism of joy. The truth is that the work God is doing in your life is greater than the forces at work against you.

Mission trips always provide an opportunity to put this principle into practice. Whether it is making your way through airport security, dealing with changing schedules, caring for injured team members, managing conflict or any myriad of problems, mission trips are fertile ground for obstacles to invade your space. In those moments, we can get frustrated with a pouty lip and furrowed brows because there is plenty justification for discouragement, but the truth is that obstacles also provide the opportunity for greater dependence on the Lord. After all, the trip belongs to Him not us. Obstacles also set the tone for greater unity and bonding within the team. I have learned to welcome, embrace, and rejoice in the challenges presented on mission trips because the good that comes out of them is greater than the discomfort they cause.

In the believer's life, joy is not an effect, it is a cause.

Do you want peace? Rejoice always!

The second element Paul gives is to be gentle (v. 5). In the ESV, it is translated "Let your reasonableness be known to everyone." How many times have you approached someone and said, "Dear sir, I would appreciate it if you would let your reasonableness be made known?" We don't talk that way today, but the intent of the word is to be gentle.

Remember, we are talking about obtaining the promise of peace amid life's turmoil. It seems a bit strange for Paul to say that one of the key ingredients to this peace formula is to be gentle. But is it really?

When I was young, I used to cut a hole in the top of an orange, turn that juicy fruit upside down, position it right over my open mouth, and squeeze it as hard as I could. That quenching juice flowed out of that orange and tasted *so* good. To be honest, I never did that with a lemon. Yeah, I love lemonade, but that is after that lemon juice has been doctored up with some sweetener. By itself, lemon juice is just too tart for a full-on squeeze into the mouth.

When life's difficulties squeeze us, what comes out of us? Often when times get tough, our demeanor gets rough. I saw this humorous meme other day:

> # Me: Don't try me
> # Them: But I thought you were a Christian
> # Me: I am, but I'm from the south side of the kingdom 😂😂😂

That is funny because most of us have felt those days, right? But sadly, the transference of our frustrations comes across as lashing out on those closest to us. Sometimes, it is transferred to those who are watching us for evidence if what we say we believe is true.

Galatians 5:22-23 gives the fruit of the Spirit. This fruit constitutes the characteristics that we bear when we are plugged into the Vine (John 15). The Spirit produces the fruit; we bear the fruit. Another way to put it is that when we are walking in the Spirit and we get squeezed, these are the things that will come out of us. Guess what one of those fruits is: yep, gentleness.

This is not a call to perfection. We are all going to have times where we mess up and lose it. However, these types of responses are not going to bring about peace. Peace is found when we can manage our temperament despite the pressures. This gentleness is found in abiding in the Vine.

Do you want peace? Be intentionally gentle even when you are getting pressed.

The third element in the prescription for peace is to not worry (v. 6). Yeah, I know. That is easy to say and hard to put into practice. Before we start to justify our worry, let's acknowledge that this is a command. Jesus makes this command 3 times in the Sermon on the Mount (Matthew 6). This is not a suggestion or wish; it is a command. This means that rejecting worry is expected from the follower of Jesus. It also means that He gives us the strength to do just that.

How often do we consume our thoughts with things that we cannot control? Many times, we find no peace in our lives because we refuse to release the very things that are blocking that peace.

Everything we worry about in life will fall into one of two categories: things we can control and things we cannot. There is no sense in worrying about either one. We should not worry about things we can control—just control it! We should not worry about things we cannot control—just release it! Why do we hold onto the things we cannot control? We beg God to pry them from our white-knuckled hands, while at the same time never releasing them.

"Humble yourselves, therefore, under the mighty hand of God so that at the proper time he may exalt you, casting all your anxieties on him, because he cares for you" (1 Peter 5:6-7). Humble yourself in this context insinuates that we need to quit trying to be god in our own lives. Give the things to God that we can't control and only He can.

Do you want peace? Trust God. Release your worry. Breathe.

The final element in this prescription is to pray (v. 6). I love the way that Paul puts this command. We let our request be made to God. We tell God what He already knows but we still need to say, what we need to recognize. When do we do this? In everything, not just the bad times or just the good.

And do not forget to do so with thanksgiving. That's right. In a similar way to rejoicing, thanksgiving becomes a step, not a response. It is somewhat easy to be thankful for what God has done. However, here we are challenged to be thankful before we even see the result. Pray in a spirit of thankfulness. This is called faith. This type of praying is full-on faith. It is not a faith that God will do exactly what we want. It is a faith that no matter what the results are, they will bring about God's glory and our good.

Prayer is not about dictating to God what He needs to do. We sometimes treat God as a heavenly ATM where we go to withdraw blessings for our benefit. Or we treat Him like a puppet on a string Who is obligated to move in the ways we direct. That is not the purpose of prayer. Prayer draws us in line with His will, not the other way around.

A boat that casts its rope to land is not pulling the land closer to the boat. It is pulling the boat closer to the immovable land. Prayer functions in the same way. It is not about getting God in line with me, it about getting imperfect me closer to the perfect God.

Do you want peace? Pray about everything with humble thanksgiving.
Rejoice. Be gentle. Do not worry. Pray.

Then what? Verse seven says: "And the peace of God, which surpasses all understanding, will guard your hearts and your minds in Christ Jesus."

What a promise! The peace of God can't even be understood or fully explained. Have you ever experienced that kind of peace? It is the kind of calmness of heart in the midst of storms that you can't even describe to someone else. It is *all* God. It is that kind of peace that is promised. And it is a vigilant peace. It sets up a sentry to guard your heart and mind. The heart is the seat of the emotions. The mind is the center of our thinking. Our emotions and thoughts are where this indescribable peace is needed and that is exactly where it is promised.

Peace is not a pipe dream or far-off desire or unreasonable wish. "The Lord is at hand." (Philippians 4:5) Now go get it.

CHAPTER 9

THE HOLY THOUGHT-SIFTER

THE COMBINATION OF THE ROOSTER CROWING, MY alarm going off, and some early risers talking all came together to force me out of a sweaty sleep and welcome me into a new day in Honduras. My team was there on a mission trip building a couple of classrooms for a church in this remote village.

For that day, my role was to make concrete that would be placed between the blocks of the building. There was not a powered concrete mixer in this region; I was the mixer! I was connected to a shovel all day long. The process for making the mud was as follows: first, a big pile of dirt had to be sifted through a wooden, rectangle frame lined with a metal mesh screen, built at a 90° angle. I shoveled dirt through the sifter which separated out rock and other unwanted elements. The next step was to take the refined sand and shovel it into a pile that resembled a volcano. Then we mixed concrete powder in with the sand. It took me a while to get the hang of the mixing motion. Scoop in, lift, twist, dump. Repeat. Once mixed up, we made a hole in the middle of the volcano and begin filling it with water following that same mixing motion with the shovel. After much sweat, blisters, back pain, and perseverance, we had concrete. We repeated this process over and over throughout the day. Several times I squeezed enough sweat out my headband to fill a moderate cup. Someone said to me, "Bill, it looks like that shovel is your best friend today."

I replied, "Best friends don't treat you like that!"

To have an eternal perspective, it is imperative that we treat our thoughts like that dirt on the sifter. We need to take a big old shovel to every thought that comes to mind and toss that thought upon the "Holy Sifter." We should only keep and hold onto the thoughts that make it through the sifter.

2 Corinthians 10:4-5 states: "For the weapons of our warfare are not of the flesh but have divine power to destroy strongholds. We destroy arguments and every lofty opinion raised against the knowledge of God, and take every thought captive to obey Christ," Taking captive every thought indicates seizing thoughts, doing a thorough pat-down and examination. Then you release and allow the thoughts that hold up to God's standard, the ones that don't get thrown in the slammer.

The peace of God that the Word promises us in Philippians 4:7 is set up to guard our hearts and minds in Christ Jesus. Now Paul goes further and tells his readers to make choices on what they focus their minds on.

I had no control over the pile of dirt I inherited that hot day in Honduras. However, I had a choice on what I did with that pile. We may not always be able to control the thoughts that come into our minds, but we can make choices on what we do with them.

"If then you have been raised with Christ, seek the things that are above, where Christ is, seated at the right hand of God. *Set your minds on things that are above, not on things that are on earth.* For you have died, and your life is hidden with Christ in God" (Colossians 3:1-3 *italics mine*).

This is not some self-help, positive thinking formula. This is Spirit-empowered mastering of the mind. Our minds are infected with a sinful, selfish nature; however, as believers, they have been redeemed by the Spirit. This is not something you just talk yourself out of, you must be submitted to and filled with the Holy Spirit.

The best way to get rid of the harmful thoughts is not to try your best to eliminate those thoughts. The best way is to fill your mind with the truth of the Word. So, on what are we to train our minds to focus? Paul asserts eight exemplary thoughts worthy of our attention in Philippians 4:8. These are the materials by which the thought sifter is built.

What makes up the sifter?

Think on whatever is **TRUE**...not false (or unknown). Ask yourself: "Are these thoughts accurate?" Sometimes what you think is true isn't. Our perception, especially when we are judging the thoughts and intent of someone else, can be skewed. Thoughts spent on inaccurate understanding is wasted time. Don't presume that you automatically know the truth of a situation. Investigate. Only hold onto the things that are true *(Ephesians 4:25-27)*.

Think on whatever is **HONORABLE**...not dishonorable. Ask yourself: "Are these thoughts honest? Are they admirable?" There is no greater call than to bring honor and glory to the One who gave His all for us. His honor and glory should be at the forefront of this filter for our thoughts. If it does not exalt Him, then cast it aside *(Revelation 4:9-11)*.

Think on whatever is **JUST**...not unjust. Ask yourself: "Are they right? Are they more about preference or God's justice?" Sometimes our thoughts have nothing to do with the righteousness of God, but about our own desires or expectations. We get angry when we do not get our way. Righteous anger is not self-centered but is focused on the glory of God and the plight of the helpless. Examine why you are you angry and see if it measures up to the righteous standard of God *(Deuteronomy 10:17-21)*.

Think on whatever is **PURE**...not impure. Ask yourself: "Are these thoughts clean or impure? Do they make you feel clean or dirty?" We wash our bodies to get them clean. We use hand sanitizer to eliminate harmful bacteria. Whether the thoughts are envious, greedy, lustful, hateful, etc., we need to wash them with the cleansing purifier of God's Word *(Psalm 24:3-6)*.

Think on whatever is **LOVELY**...not repulsive. Ask yourself: "Are these thoughts going to bring a smile to your face and glow to your heart? Are they going to make you recoil?" Every time my wife looks at the beach her facial expression exclaims loveliness. Every time my wife looks at the alarm clock when it goes off at 5am her facial expression exclaims disgust. Think on the lovely thoughts *(Psalm 96:1-6)*.

Think on whatever is **COMMENDABLE**...not wrong. Ask yourself: "Are these thoughts regarding good report or bad report? Are they worth repeating?" We can be so quick to believe the worst about someone. We can crave the juicy gossip and the meaty details. But these dishonorable thoughts are not honoring to the One who loves every person that we gawk at in disgust. *(James 3:15-18)*

Think on anything that is **EXCELLENT**...not filthy. Ask yourself: "Are these thoughts extolling the virtuous characteristics of God or settling for the deceit of self?" We are often experts at justifying our sins. However, there is no justification for sin. We deceive ourselves when we entreat our minds towards the worthless works of the flesh rather than the excellence of our Lord *(James 1:14-18)*.

Think on anything that is **WORTHY OF PRAISE**...not shameful. Ask yourself: "Are these thoughts building up or tearing down? Are these thoughts causing rejoicing or regret?" Thoughts that extol the worst in others or our circumstances should be rejected. It can be easy for us to see the negative in any given situation. I have to admit, it is difficult for me to hang around people who can find the absolute worst in even the best context. It's not about just having a positive attitude; it is about having a Christ-attitude *(Philippians 2:5)*.

Romans 8:5-7 says,

"For those who live according to the flesh set their minds on the things of the flesh, but *those who live according to the Spirit set their minds on the things of the Spirit*. For to set the mind on the flesh is death, but to set the mind on the Spirit is life and peace. For the mind that is set on the flesh is hostile to God, for it does not submit to God's law; indeed, it cannot" *(Italics mine).*

It all makes sense. A mind set on things of the flesh is a mind focused on death and the temporary. A mind set on things of the Spirit is a mind focused on life, peace, and the eternal.

As important as it is to send your thoughts through the sifter, you still have to act on it. It was one thing to get the sand clear of impurities, but it didn't matter if it just sat there unused. I still had to use it to make the concrete.

Paul, therefore, finishes this passage with a call to put these things into practice. James proclaimed a similar sentiment when he wrote:

"But be doers of the word, and not hearers only, deceiving yourselves. For if anyone is a hearer of the word and not a doer, he is like a man who looks intently at his natural face in a mirror. For he looks at himself and goes away and at once forgets what he was like. But the one who looks into the perfect law, the law of liberty, and perseveres, being no hearer who forgets but a doer who acts, he will be blessed in his doing." –James 1:22-25

Paul challenged the people to practice what they had learned. In other words, they should increase in knowledge through its use and practice. Knowledge is one thing. Wisdom is the proper use of knowledge. Most people I counsel are not suffering through lack of knowledge. It is the lack of practical application of that knowledge that gets them in trouble. We must not just know the truth; we must live it.

Paul encouraged them to act on what they had received. To receive was to accept or embrace what they had been given. They took the truth to heart. We also need to fully embrace the grace of God, allowing it to infiltrate our minds and hearts. This reception changes everything.

Paul urged them to move on what they had heard and seen. They were to perceive, understand and correctly interpret what they experienced. We too must let the Word of God be the lens by which we see the events going on around us. We let God's Word interpret our circumstances, not the other way around.

David alluded to this in 1 Chronicles 22:17-19. He basically is telling the leaders to open their eyes to what God has done around them. The presence of the Lord is evident if they would open their eyes. Then he commands them to "set your mind and heart to seek the Lord God." (v. 19) This setting of the mind and heart would lead to action.

Have you ever had a song stuck in your head? I had a great team with me one year on a mission trip to Moldova. But every time we got in the vans to go somewhere someone would break into the song "Baby Shark," with all of the verses! I got so tired of that song, yet I would wake up in the morning with that song on my mind. Ugh! The only way to get that song out of my head on that trip was to sing a new song.

So, there you have it. Want to get rid of that depressing, fearful, angry, discontented, envious, hateful, song replaying in your head? Sing a new song, one built on the awesome glory, grace, and gospel of our Lord Jesus. Pick up your shovel and get to sifting, my friend.

CHAPTER 10

THE HEART OF SERVICE

I DON'T KNOW IF YOU HAVE EVER EXPERIENCED AN orphanage in an impoverished country, but it is no delightful walk in the park. The conditions in these places can often be very dismal. The dirt, smells, and the darkness is heartbreaking. Children may have 2-3 outfits total. It can be a bit off-setting if you have not been to one before. The first time I was in an international orphanage I was with a team led by an evangelist.

As much as I was in culture shock at the setting, I was more impacted by this guy's actions. He stood to the side as the children gathered. He waited until a photographer showed up and then he bent down, put his arm around a child, and gave a photo-op for his news-letter. After that, he took off. Now, I am not throwing this guy under the bus. What do I know? Maybe he was having severe intestinal tur-moil and had to make a quick exit. I can't judge motives or intentions. However, I decided in that moment, right then and there, that I would never do that. I would embrace the dirt to be the hands and feet of Jesus.

I watched the kids playing and focused on one of their hand jives they were doing to see if I could learn it. I stepped out in the middle of them and put my hands out. They were skeptical of this big, bald, fat American, but one brave kid finally stepped up and accepted the invi-tation to do that hand jive. Then it was on! For the next hour, it was straight up hand slapping. Those hands were filthy and full of germs; however, at the same time, they were so beautiful.

Now, I haven't necessarily always jumped into the mix. I have had my times of holding back and staying to the side. I have had my moments of shrinking back for one reason or another. But I have never regretted getting involved and serving hand to hand. At an orphanage in Moldova, I started making balloon animals. The kids crowded in on me to where I could barely move. They were sneezing and coughing like crazy. When I got back from that trip, I brought with me an unintended and unwanted souvenir: an upper respiratory infection. It leveled me for over a week, and I had a cough for literally a year. Obviously, I would regret that contact, right? Actually, no. I would do it again for the opportunity to show the love of Jesus to least of these. I always tell my mission teams to jump in there and get involved. You can wash the "blessings" off later. Sure, use Purell. Don't touch your dirty hands to your mouth.[4] But don't let the mess keep you out of the mix.

Jesus modeled this so beautifully in John 13. He has gathered with the disciples in the upper room on the Thursday before the crucifixion. In a few short hours He would be arrested. So, these were His last few moments with His band of brothers before the dreadful events that lay ahead. He packed these last few hours with some powerful teaching and prayers (John 14-17). However, in chapter 13, it is not His words but His actions that speak volumes.

As they were eating dinner, Jesus knew what was to come. He got up from the table, stripped down and tied a towel around his waist. He filled a basin with water, knelt and started washing the feet of His disciples and drying them with a towel.

These were not feet fresh off a pedicure, powdered and fragranced. No, these were normal feet one would find in that region 2000 years

---

4 My good friend Donald Gillette is a missionary in Nicaragua. He has a famous quote for the teams he hosts, "Don't ever touch your fingers to your lips or you shall surely die!"

ago. They were dirty feet that had been strapped up in sandals. They no doubt had caked-on dirt and grime from walking. It that culture, it was common to have someone wash people's feet when they would come in a house so as not to track in dirt. This was seen as a pretty lowly responsibility.

In this gathering place, where the disciples were all ears, they were not exactly all hands. Nobody was interested in cleaning feet. Jesus used the setting as the perfect scenario to teach them a valuable lesson they would need to learn if they were to represent Him after He left this earth.

Oh, how cool it would have been to be there observing the disciples' faces as Jesus displayed this incredible act of humility. Imagine the whispered conversations He may have had as he knelt before each unworthy brother. The King of kings and Lord of lords, the Creator of the universe had taken on the role of a servant washing feet. Everyone breathing in that room that night must have been in shock as he gently cleansed each foot. Utterly astounding.

To bring even more perspective to this self-denial, He washed the feet of Judas, the one who would betray Him. It was not until after this display that Judas left to go do His devilish deed. Yet, John makes it clear that Jesus knows all about what Judas is up to before He washes feet. If it had been me, I would have told Judas to make sure the door didn't hit him on the way out *before* I knelt down to do some foot massaging. But I'm not Jesus. He actually *served* His betrayer.

How could He do that? It's easy for us to say, "But that's Jesus! No one can expect me to treat my enemies with that type of kindness. Only Jesus could do that." Making an excuse like that overlooks some crucial observations. First, it is the truth of who Jesus is that makes this act so irrational. He is God the Son. He is the One who should be bowed down to, adored, and lavishly served. Yet, He humbles Himself. We have no standing of greatness on our own. Apart from Christ, we are just as miserable and wicked and lost as those who seek our downfall.

Secondly, this same Jesus actually instructs us to serve in the same way. Look at what Jesus said after He had finished this service.

> "Do you understand what I have done to you? You call me Teacher and Lord, and you are right, for so I am. If I then, your Lord and Teacher, have washed your feet, you also ought to wash one another's feet. For I have given you an example, that you also should do just as I have done to you. Truly, truly, I say to you, a servant is not greater than his master, nor is a messenger greater than the one who sent him." –John 13:12-16

Remember what Jesus instructed at the Sermon on the Mount:

> "You have heard that it was said, 'You shall love your neighbor and hate your enemy.' But I say to you, Love your enemies and pray for those who persecute you, so that you may be sons of your Father who is in heaven. For he makes his sun rise on the evil and on the good, and sends rain on the just and on the unjust." –Matthew 5:43-45

Serving others in the name of Jesus is not limited to those whom we like and who like us. It is not even limited to those who appreciate it. We must adopt the eternal perspective of Jesus and understand that we serve because we have *been* served. We give of ourselves because He *gave Himself* for us. We reach out because He *reached down* to us. The love and example and glory of Jesus are the ultimate motivations for serving others.

Before we move on from this passage, we do need to touch on Peter's conversation with Jesus during the foot-washing. As seen throughout the gospels, Peter had a way of letting his mouth get ahead of his brain. Have you ever known someone like that? Have you ever been someone like that? I think we can all relate to Peter on one level or another. On this occasion, Peter chastises Jesus. "You shall never wash my feet" (v. 8). This statement was most likely produced from a heart that felt unworthy of such a display from His Lord. The problem is that Peter was telling his Lord what to do. Jesus, in His patience says, "Ok Peter, if that is the case, then we will have nothing to do with each other from here on out" (my paraphrase). Peter again steps out and tells Jesus what to do, "Lord, not my feet but also my hands and my head!" (v. 9). Good grief, Peter! Just close your mouth for a moment and let Jesus do what He is going to do.

Good grief, Bill! Just close your mouth for a moment and let Jesus do what He is going to do.

Go ahead, put your name in there. How often do we jump out there and instruct the omniscient One on what He needs to do? How often do we create justifications for what we *want* to do? How often do we create excuses for not doing what God has called us to do?

We can come up with a multitude of reasons to hold back from serving others, but none of them will eliminate the one reason that we should: He told us to follow His example and serve others in love.

There are some individuals at my church who may never be up on stage. They don't want it; they serve behind the scenes. When all the people have walked out of worship and left behind their water bottles, paper coffee cups, candy wrappers, and used tissues, these guys are on the scene. They brandish trash bags and keen eyesight. To my knowledge, they have never been asked to take on that role. They just do it. One of them once told me when we moved into our new building, God clearly impressed upon his heart that he was to take care of that place so God's work could be done well there. Wow! No applause. No recognition. No social media posts—these guys would probably be highly embarrassed that I am mentioning them here—what they *do* have is a trash bag coupled with a heart and a passion for service.

Whether you are praying over someone, picking up trash, making a balloon animal, hugging someone dirty, or engaging in countless other ways to share the love of Jesus and His gospel, give it all you got. Some blessings you can wash off and some you will never want to. But in the end, when it is all said and done, the service done in His name will all be worth it, because He is worthy.

Section 3:

"For this light momentary affliction is preparing for us an eternal weight of glory beyond all comparison..."

CHAPTER 11

THE HOLY TAPESTRY

A T THE TIME I AM WRITING THIS BOOK, THERE ARE approximately 195 countries in the world containing 7.8 billion people. Each of these individuals speak at least one of about 6,500 known languages in the world.[5] Yet throughout all of those languages, there are three words that are the same regardless of the countries or cultures I have personally experienced. When I go on mission trips, I always take the opportunity to point out these three words. The first is "Amen!" It may be pronounced a little differently, but it is the same everywhere. The second is "Hallelujah!" The third, which is a little lesser known, but still significant is "BoomShakaLaka!" Ok, so that last one is one I have highjacked and taken around the world, but it is so fun to say. I can tell you that once kids catch on to the craziness, which can sometimes take a bit, they love responding to that word! Interestingly, in Moldova, I was told that it sounded a lot like their word for chocolate, which may explain why kids expected me to have some sweets to give them.

Given the multitude of differences in cultures I have experienced in the world, there are still many things that are the same. People love to laugh. People respond to love. In addition, genuine Christians are passionate about their faith. These similarities especially stand out even

---

[5] http://worldpopulationreview.com Accessed September 27, 2019.

more in oppressive cultures. Persecution actually ignites faith in true believers.

Recently, I was on a mission with my friend to China to train church leaders covertly. China has long been a hotbed of Christian persecution. Government propaganda will assert religious tolerance; however, there is a *big* asterisk to that assertion. China has a state-run church called the "Three-Self" church. These are really the only native churches that can legally meet in China.[6] Ultimately in a communist system, the powers that be desire for citizens to bow to the government above all. That principle drives the government to sponsor a church that it can control. Just recently, these Three-Self churches were ordered to remove the 10 Commandments from their facilities and replace them with direct quotes from the president of China. These quotes highlight core socialist values, which are also inserted into the Chinese version of the Bible that is approved by the government.[7]

Most of the churches in China are not Three-Self, but are Bible-believing, Christ-honoring, and gospel-proclaiming. They are also underground, which means that they do not meet in public places. Church leaders in China face various levels of persecution depending on the mood and perspective of the local government officials. In parts of the nation, these Christians are aggressively sought out and imprisoned—or worse.

In the particular town we were in, these underground churches were somewhat tolerated as long as they kept to themselves. Regardless of the demeanor of the government officials toward the Chinese church, one thing they do come against is religious teaching from outsiders,

---

[6] In an effort to capitulate to the West and its money, churches for non-Chinese people are often legal. However, many times government officials will scout these churches looking for any native Chinese citizens. If they find any, they will be removed and subject to penalties under the law. I learned this from Dr. William Wilson who taught in China for 6 years.

[7] https://www.lifesitenews.com/news/china-orders-ten-commandments-re-placed-with-communist-leaders-quotes Accessed September 27, 2019.

which is what we were doing. Gratefully, in this storefront setting, we had no issues as we strived to pour into these leaders.

My first trip to Vietnam was similar. The communist government decided in 2008 to legalize evangelical churches. That means it allowed churches to register with local governments and achieve official status. This legalization governed corporate meetings on Sunday but still made it illegal to openly share the gospel publicly. However, as long as the local government officials were amiable, Christians could meet without fear of persecution. That fact, though, did not stop government officials from following me around the country in 2010 as I trained pastors and taught at churches. While it was a bit unnerving, I found great satisfaction in knowing that these officials were sitting under the proclamation of God's Word. Regardless of intent, they were hearing the Word!

That activity has been a passion of mine from nation to nation. From the United States to Brazil, Honduras to China, Vietnam to Nicaragua, India to Moldova, training pastors has been an incredible privilege and joy in my life.

I have had people challenge my sensibility before. Why would I take the risks that come with international travel to train pastors? I have some health issues that put me at greater risk. Why would I go into areas where Christians are being persecuted? I have a Christian faith that puts me at greater risk in those countries. There are several reasons. First, these Christians are my fellow believers in Christ. They are my brothers and sisters. They face persecution or obstacles on a daily basis of which a typical American has no concept. Why would I not take a bit of my time to step into their context and bring some encouragement, training, and truth? When a particular mission trip is done, I am usually spent and worn-out. But it is the perfect kind of exhaustion, the kind that comes with the satisfaction and encouragement of fulfilling a calling. In addition, I cannot overstate the joy it brings to fellowship with the faithful.

The second reason I go is because of the influential position pastors have. Most of these pastors have the passion but little training. Their churches are looking to them for spiritual guidance and they are giving their best. Why would I walk away from an opportunity to increase their best? Pastors influence churches. Churches influence communities. Communities influence nations.

Finally, I go because we need to keep before us the true magnitude of God's church worldwide. If we neglect stepping into other cultures, we keep a narrow focus. We drift toward thinking that God's primary language is English, heaven looks a whole lot like my immediate culture. and Jesus is a pale-skinned, long-haired, blue-eyed European. These are total misperceptions.

Listen to the palmist in Psalm 67 (emphasis mine):

> May God be gracious to us and bless us and make his
> face to shine upon us, Selah
> that your way may be known *on earth*, your saving
> power *among the nations*
> Let the peoples praise you, O God; let *all the peoples*
> praise you!
> *Let the nations* be glad and sing for joy, for you judge
> *the peoples with equity* and guide *the nations upon the*
> *earth*. Selah
> Let the peoples praise you, O God; let *all the peoples*
> praise you! *The earth* has yielded its increase; God, our
> God, shall bless us.
> God shall bless us; let *all the ends of the earth* fear him!

You cannot read that Psalm without realizing that our God is the God of the nations. He has a heart for the entire earth to proclaim His way, to display His power, to bring gladness and joy, to judge equitably, to bring blessings, and to draw people to praise and fear Him. If His heart is for the nations, how can we ignore them?

God does a beautiful thing when He weaves together His holy tapestry. A tapestry is a fabric consisting of a multitude of different colored threads that are usually woven together by hand producing a pictorial design. My wife and I were recently touring the Vatican Museum in Rome. The hallways were filled with huge, elaborate tapestries depicting biblical events. It truly was amazing, especially considering how much time this must have taken the artists to create.

Here's the thing: if you were to look at one of these tapestries from behind, it may look like a jumbled mess. If the picture is even discernible, it would be out of focus, with distorted edges and lines. But all that disorder comes into focus on the other side.

You likely can see where I am going with this. Sometimes being in different cultures with different languages and customs can be a little overwhelming. It can certainly be confusing. That discomfort is what we see on the backside of the tapestry. *An eternal perspective* carries you around to the other side of the tapestry, the side where the picture comes into clear view. This is where you see God bringing His people together from every tongue and every nation.

I have stood in worship services where I could not understand anything that was being said. I have also been with fellow believers where I knew enough of their language to pick up a word here or there. However, I don't have to know all the words to experience the worship. The bond that the Holy Spirit can create which crosses over those languages and cultures is miraculous. Every time I am in one of these worship settings with other believers from different nationalities, I am reminded of the greatness of our God. What an incredible blessing it is to experience this kind of fellowship that can only be explained by the Spirit!

God is not American, Chinese, Brazilian, Iranian, or even Israeli. He is the God of the nations who made a promise to Abraham to bless the world through his seed. He used Israel to usher in the Savior for the world, light breaking into the darkness.

An *eternal perspective* recognizes that nationalities are temporary, and His kingdom is eternal. As believers, our allegiance is first and foremost to our eternal home. I can hear someone challenge me: "So, you're not proud to be an American?" Let me carefully state it like this:

> I am very grateful to be an American and a recipient of the many blessings that we have as Americans, which are unmatched in the parts of the world I have experienced. I recognize as a believer in Jesus Christ that I do belong to this temporal world, but my *home* is heaven. Therefore, I will view the blessings I have received, not as assets to be hoarded, but as resources to further the eternal kingdom which will be inhabited by all those who profess faith in Jesus Christ, from every nation, culture, and language.

All praise to the God of the nations, Creator of the most beautiful tapestry you will ever lay eyes on. BoomShakaLaka!

CHAPTER 12

WHOSE BOY IS HE

M Y DAD MARRIED MY MOM AND ADOPTED ME when I was 5 years old. As God would have it, my Dad and I kind of look like one another. I remember one time when I was a young man, my Dad and I were at an event. Someone made a comment to my Dad that was something like this: "Boy, you can't deny that he is your son. Y'all look just alike."

I will never forget looking into the eyes of this man who made a choice to call me his own and him giving me a slight wink. That small, intentional twitch of the eye carried a ton of communication. This was our little secret. Nobody else had to know that his genetic code did not flow through my body. Nobody had to know the years and experiences that had brought us to where we were that day. Nope. My Dad just looked at the man, chuckled, and said, "I know it." It was true after all: I was his and he would never deny me.

Evidently, however, the genes I do carry within me are quite strong. My wife and I joke about how she did the majority of the work in birthing our kids and yet they came out looking like me. One of my best friends, who happens to be a master at creating nicknames, came up with "special" names for my kids. He called my son "Small Bill." For my daughter he chose "Bill-Face." Thankfully, those nicknames did not stick! Nobody would ever choose to be called Bill-Face after me! But I can't deny the fact that they do favor me in the looks department...that said, they make "me" look good.

As parents, we take the responsibility of raising babies to adults very seriously. Parents experience moments of indecision and second-guessing. We understand the weight of cradling that special treasure and gift in our arms. We have spent sleepless nights holding, cuddling, cleaning up puke, playing games, and begging them to go back night-night. We have cried at Kindergarten drop-offs, yelled (sometimes out of encouragement, sometimes out of frustration) at ball games, and cleaned up cuts and scrapes. We have helped with their homework, prayed with them over their worries, and done a majority of their science projects. We endured the middle school years and praised the Lord when they were redeemed from that cesspool environment of changing bodies and hateful words.

We rejoiced in those moments when each one approached us about placing their faith in Christ. Trying to keep our emotions at bay so that we would not manipulate them, we questioned them to see if their understanding of the gospel was accurate. The days I baptized my children are some of the most significant in my life. Those days approach the brilliance of that day back on June 18, 1994, when the doors swung open, and I saw my bride walking down the aisle in that stunning dress. She was as close as one can come to being cast with a backlit illumination of a halo over her head—at least that is what I remember. Seeing my kids come out of the waters of baptism, hearing the applause of their brothers and sisters in Christ, and witnessing the ear-to-ear smile on their faces—well, these are the moments you dream about. It is really hard to describe how sweet it is to drink in that cocktail of pride, joy, and peace.

Then before you know it, this journey of parenthood takes a sharp, dangerous, and disheartening curve. I saw the sign coming long before it happened. Slow Down! Curve Ahead! Lights flashing: Dangerous Speed! Nevertheless, I didn't put the brakes on soon enough and the curve still made me feel like I was losing control, careening off the road. It was more than a feeling, I was *actually* losing control of my kids.

No sign or instruction from others can prepare you for when you drop your "kid" off at college and drive away. All the upbringing and instilling of values and molding of faith now enter a different phase. The tilling, planting, and fertilizing part is done. Now we have to wait and see what grows out of the soil of preparation. Watching my son walk away from me on that college campus was like seeing my own heart ripped out of my chest and moving on without me.

I am reminded of when Jesus' family had attended the Passover festivities in Jerusalem. (Luke 2:41-52) When the feast had ended, they headed home. They didn't see Jesus, but they were traveling as a big group, so they thought their 12-year-old was hanging out with the other adolescents.[8] After a day had passed, they began to get worried when no one could find Him. Have you ever had those moments of panic when you lost track of your kid for a brief time? Multiply that emotion for the parents of the Savior of the world! He was apart from them for *5 days total* and where did they find Him? Curled up in the corner of the street? Crying at the local police station? Skateboarding in the park with His homies? No. They found him at the temple, the holy site in Jerusalem. The Bible says He amazed folks as He was "sitting among the teachers, listening to them, and asking them questions."[9] (Luke 2:47) When Joseph and Mary approached Him, they were a little perturbed, to say the least. You know that mixture of relief and

---

[8] The very fact that they had this perception gives us a little insight into the presumed normal-ness of His upbringing. The Word records very little about the years between His birth and His ministry. Why were they not paranoid, keeping Him under their wing at all times? Most likely, because He was a normal boy who hung out and played with His friends.

[9] This is really amazing. His approach here is notable and instructive to us. He is sitting among the teachers. He is not only teaching them, but He is listening to them and asking questions. So much to unpack here but will have to let this little note suffice for now!

frustration, like when you yank your kid out of the road moments before a car passes, you are relieved that he did not get hurt but you are a little ticked that he was in that position in the first place.

Here, the parents had lost the Son of God. When they found Him, they felt a little justified to scold Him. They basically accused Him of treating them poorly and that He had put them through a great deal of stress. He seemed a little confused at their grief. Why didn't they automatically look for Him at the temple? They, of all people, knew the miraculous circumstances of His birth. They, more than anyone, knew who He was. They certainly should know His purpose for being here. He was the *Messiah*! But no, in that moment, they did not understand.

So, what does Jesus do? Ignore them? Keep teaching? Tell them to bug off? Nope. The adolescent King of kings, Creator of the universe, Alpha and Omega, packed up His stuff, submitted to their temporal authority, and headed back with them. Wow! That is simply amazing. He just continued His path of growing both physically and mentally, preparing for the coming ministry ahead.

Fast forward about 2000 years to my son, Austin. It is his junior year in college, and he calls to tell us he is going to be baptized at the church he attends. Beg your pardon? The conversation went something like this:

Me: "Ok. Why do you want to be re-baptized?"

Him: "I didn't know what I was doing when I did it at 9."

Me: "I'm pretty sure you did. We talked at length. As much as a 9-year-old could understand, you knew. I am sure of it."

Him: "Well, I know a lot more now and have grown in my faith. This gives me an opportunity to share my story and celebrate with my current church family

Me: "We'll be there."

I had an internal battle with my pride and emotions. I thought, *so I baptized my son, but he doesn't recognize that anymore? He didn't start growing in his faith until college? No way I'm believing that! I lived with him and saw growth over 18 years.* Nevertheless, this was a significant moment in his life, we had been invited, and we were not going to miss it.

That Sunday, they played his video testimony before he was baptized. He spoke in it about how his faith came alive after he started attending this church in college. There was no mention of his pastor-father, his godly mother, or the faith-infused gospel-saturated upbringing we gave him. He simply went into the water, came up, and the place erupted with cheers and his best buddies surrounded him. I clapped on the outside—inside was a little different. It brought me great joy to see him so embraced by others and for him to proclaim his faith, but I honestly felt a little slighted. *So, all my investment over the years meant nothing. Hmph.*

After the baptisms, we sang the song "Who You Say I Am." That song says:

> "Who the Son sets free
> Oh is free indeed
> I'm a child of God
> Yes I am
> In my Father's house
> There's a place for me
> I'm a child of God
> Yes I am"[10]

As I sang that song, God wrecked me. He weighed heavy on my heart and I felt Him saying repeatedly: "Bill, who do you want your son to love more: Me or you?"

As tears welled up in my eyes and emotion captured my heart, I prayed:

---

[10] Hillsong Worship, *There is More*, "Who You Say I Am," Capitol Christian Music Group, 2019.

Oh God, forgive me. In my pride, I wanted to be his hero. I wanted to be built up as the greatest influence in his life's story. I wanted him to speak of me with gratitude and reverence. But it's not about me. It's all about You, Jesus. My 21-year-old son is celebrating his faith with his brothers and sisters in Christ. Here, for the first time in his life, he is not the pastor's kid. He is volunteering for ministry. He is going on mission trips. He is living out his faith on his terms and in his way. Who do I think I am to make this about me?

Yes, Lord. I want him to love You more than me
Yes, Lord. I want him to serve You more than me
Yes, Lord, I want him to revere You more than me
Yes, Lord, I want him to communicate with You more than me.
After all, he is Your child before he is mine.

CHAPTER 13

HALL OF FAITH

RECENTLY, MY WIFE AND I CELEBRATED OUR 25TH wedding anniversary. It has been quite a journey and we do not take lightly the significance of this milestone, especially in light of how many marriages do not finish the race set before them. Surviving marriages go through all the good, bad, ugly, joys and triumphs, and the griefs and frustrations. The warm fuzzy feelings of newlywed bliss will not sustain a marriage. A pursuit of the Lord that is greater than the pursuit of your spouse is a key ingredient to a lasting marriage. Self-sacrifice and focus on meeting your spouse's needs above your own are *vital* components. Fierce commitment and unwavering perseverance are necessary. Interestingly, we were reminded of these elements on our 25th anniversary trip, albeit in an unexpected way.

For the last 5 years, we had hoped and dreamed and saved and prayed for a large anniversary trip. Tiffany loves our annual excursions to Myrtle Beach, but this milestone anniversary was calling for something more. We had our sights set on a cruise through the Greek Islands. Well, dreams do come true sometimes and, with some serious bargain hunting, we were able to make that trip become a reality: Santorini, Mykonos, Athens, and Katakolon (Olympia). It was the trip of a lifetime, being the perfect balance of relaxation and touring. As an added benefit, we got to spend a couple of days in Rome. We only got a taste of Rome with our two tours, but we did get to mark something off my bucket list: The Colosseum.

There was always something about the mystique and history of that place that has intrigued me. Now to be sure, I was never a huge fan of my history classes over the years. Unless the professor was super dynamic, I always had difficulty getting into the spirit of those historical events locked within the walls of the classroom. However, walking in history is a different ballgame altogether! To stand in the very places where these stories actually took place is exhilarating to me. So, when it came to the Colosseum and the events that took place there, not to mention the fact that I loved the movie "Gladiator," this historic site had etched itself firmly onto the bucket list. I had longed to see this place for a couple of decades.

Now before the criticism rolls in, I am fully aware of the problem with the glamorization of violence. Upward of 50,000 or more people would climb those steps of the ancient wonder to witness fighters, animals, and civilians kill each other. Squelch the rumors: I do not advocate nor enjoy killing for sport. I also acknowledge that Christ calls us to turn the other cheek. I personally have never been in a physical fight with someone (The one time an 8th grader punched me in my 6th-grader chest, and I slinked away with my head down doesn't count). However, there is something about fighting for your life that causes the warrior within to stand up and salute.

As we took the mesmerizing tour through the Colosseum, we were on information overload as our Italian guide machine-gunned historical facts our way. It was too much to take in. But one tidbit of information really made an impact. There is a cross set up on the southern side of the inner Colosseum. It is positioned in the spot where the Roman Emperor would sit during the events taking place. There were times in the events when a participant would beg for mercy and the victorious gladiator would look to the Emperor for a thumbs-up, meaning let him live, or a thumbs-down, meaning no mercy. This gesture was displayed in the "Gladiator" movie as well. It doesn't take much imagination to see the significance of the cross placed in this significant position. The one true King with the full power of life and death is Jesus, not a human Emperor.

Historians debate how many Christians were actually martyred in the Colosseum. The answer to that debate will probably never be settled. However, there is no debating the fact that many have lost their physical lives for their faith in the one true God of the Bible. Genuine faith goes to the limit. Those characteristics of marriages that last—with Christ-pursuing, self-denial, focus, and perseverance—are the same type of characteristics you see in those who were martyred for their faith. They are the same characteristics you see in those who *live* by faith.

The writer of Hebrews goes through a museum of the faithful in Hebrews 11. Just as in museums today, one would be wise to walk slowly through, examining each exhibit. He extols the faith displayed in Old Testament believers going all the way back to the early days of humanity. The faithful who are mentioned in Hebrews 11:4-22 are all found in the book of Genesis. Verses 23-29 cover Exodus-Deuteronomy. Verses 30-31 notes the events of Joshua. Then the author mentions some prominent leaders from Judges along with prophet Samuel and King David from 1 & 2 Samuel. Each of these lives recorded had his or her own faith journey. None of them were perfect. They all had flaws, yet their faith persevered.

In Hebrews 11:33-38, he gives a list of victories on display and victories undercover, meaning those victories that on the outside look like defeats. Of these precious believers, the writer commends them as those "of whom the world was not worthy." Yet the common thread through all of these Old Testament believers was that they were extolled for their faith in a promise that they never received, at least while here on earth. That promise was Jesus (See Hebrews 12:1-2).

The way they lived with victorious faith had everything to do with an eternal perspective. Look at what the writer gives us in verses 13-16:

> **13** *These all died in faith, not having received the things promised, but having seen them and greeted them from afar, and having acknowledged that they were strangers and exiles on the earth.* **14** *For people who speak thus make it clear that they are seeking a homeland.* **15** *If they had been thinking of that land from which they had gone out, they would have had opportunity to return.* **16** *But as it is, they desire a better country, that is, a heavenly one. Therefore God is not ashamed to be called their God, for he has prepared for them a city.*

How exactly can these people have seen and greeted the things promised when they had never received them? In other words, how could they see what they were not seeing? That is the mysterious beauty of the eternal perspective.

Look at how he describes this perspective. They had to fully acknowledge that this world was not their home. They were passing through. They were strangers and exiles here. They were not immigrants. They were on visas passing through. I love to travel, in case I haven't made that point already. I love other cultures. But I always love coming back home. When I am in Germany, I am not a German. I am a visiting American. Same applies for every country I go to. I can walk the soil, eat the food, and participate in the customs, but at the end of the day, I am a visitor. As believers, do we take the same approach to our lives here on earth? An eternal perspective requires viewing this place we live through the lens of forever. This is not our home.

The writer makes it clear that if this earth was their home, they certainly could go back to where they came from. But their faith journey was more about where they were going and where they would end up than it was about embracing the temporary things of the past. This world simply would not suffice. There was better homeland coming. They would make the most of this temporal home while they lived here, but they would not lose the perspective of the eternal one that was to come. Their hope was established on the promise of the future city that God would prepare for all who would believe.

Jesus spoke to this promise in John 14, where He assured the disciples that when He left to prepare an eternal home for them, He would come again and receive them to Himself. Why? So that where He was, they would be also. That is a promise that is passed down to all who believe.

How could the martyrs and the faithful endure persecutions and death for the sake of the one true God? How can believers in hostile countries today—who worship under the daily threat of persecution and death—see their churches thriving? It is because genuine faith is believing in what has been promised even when it cannot be seen. It is because genuine faith does not fear what the world threatens nor does it embrace what the world offers; rather, everything is seen through the lens of the eternal promises of Jesus.

For the believer, the worst that life throws at you in this world is the worst it will ever get for you.

For the believer, the best that this world offers to you is rubbish compared to what is to come.

I choose to echo the shouts of those Old Testament, New Testament, and modern-day martyrs and saints: I live for a "better country, that is, a heavenly one." With that, I can boldly face anything today because my ultimate victory is certain.

CHAPTER 14

BRACE THE CORE

"BRACE YOUR CORE!**"**
Those words are a common command from my trainer. When I got serious about working out as an adult, one of the classes I would go to was called "Body Pump." This class involved a weightlifting circuit with lower weights at higher, faster-paced, repetitions. In one hour, you work out all of the major muscle groups in the body. It is probably my favorite group workout class. There was just one problem, inevitably, after a month or two, my back would start hurting and I would end up sidelined for a few months, healing up. Once I was out of the routine of going, it would be hard to get back into it. Eventually, I would return, and the cycle would start again.

I decided to check in with a trainer and see if there was anything I could do better and/or fix that I was doing wrong. This trainer put me through an assessment, and it became clear, very quickly, what my main problem was: my core was weak. The core is that part of our body that lies between our arms and our legs. It is the center part of our physical stature and it is central to most of the movements we make. My main issue was not that I was weak overall; rather, it was that I was adding strength (muscle) onto a weak core.

So, we started working on my core. That work included a lot of stability work, like lifting light weights while balancing on one leg...at the same time! I hated those exercises because it just showed how weak I really was. My trainer would constantly call out "Brace the core!" Those words had a multi-faceted effect on me. They challenged me, frustrated me, and focused me. But here's the thing: over time I began to see improvement. There were no quick fixes, but when you do it right you begin to witness increased strength.

Because my core was not strong, I had trouble with many areas, but mainly my balance. Isn't that how it often is in life? We struggle with balance in our relationships, our jobs, our schedules, our finances, and many other areas. We can also struggle with balance in our spiritual lives. When I say that, I am not meaning balance between our spiritual lives and the other aspects of our lives. When "we walk by faith, not by sight" (2 Corinthians 5:7), our lives are not compartmentalized. Everything flows in our relationship with Christ. There are not really sacred and secular categories in the life of the believer. Because we are "new creations" (2 Corinthians 5:17), and are "born again" (John 3:3), we no longer live for ourselves. Our entire lives are wrapped up in Him and through Him. As Paul stated in Galatians 2:20, "I have been crucified with Christ. It is no longer I who live, but Christ who lives in me. And the life I now live in the flesh I live by faith in the Son of God, who loved me and gave himself for me."

When I mention balance in our spiritual lives, I am really talking about the balance between grace and truth. To be clear: do not look at these two elements as being on opposite ends of the spectrum. It is not that we need a little grace and a little truth to get the balance right. To the contrary, we need both to their fullest. See them as intricately woven together in the tapestry of God's redemptive plan for man. For purposes of this concept, let me explain each one.[11]

Grace is that unearned favor of God where He delivers from condemnation all who would place their full trust in Jesus Christ as Lord and Savior. Grace places my sins upon my sinless Savior, Who took the cross for me and rose from the dead, breaking the chains of sin and death. Grace is where I get what I could never deserve or earn on my own.

Truth is that which aligns with factual reality. In the Bible, truth shows us the perfect righteousness of God and the utter sinfulness of man. Truth also incorporates the grace of God through Jesus Christ. Among other things, biblical truth tells us how we are to live, what we are to value, and what we are to discard.

Jesus is a beautiful combination of grace and truth. Look at how John puts it in John 1:14-17 *(italics mine)*:

> **14** And the Word became flesh and dwelt among us, and we have seen his glory, glory as of the only Son from the Father, *full of grace and truth*. **15** (John bore witness about him, and cried out, "This was he of whom I said, 'He who comes after me ranks before me, because he was before me.'") **16** For from his fullness we have all received, *grace upon grace*. **17** For the law was given through Moses; *grace and truth* came through Jesus Christ.

---

[11] Volumes of literature have been dedicated to the discussion about the relationship between grace and the law. I am completely aware that my handling of this subject matter will not be sufficient for a thorough handling of the subject. My primary aim is simply in how our view of grace and law impact how we process the world around through an eternal perspective. In addition, I am not stating that "truth" is all about the "law." "Truth" encompasses all things that are true, including, but not limited to, the "law."

In the lives and philosophies of many Christians, these are different. Rather than the beautiful weaving together of the two, many tend to emphasize one over the other.

Those who go to the extreme of grace roll their eyes at any biblical commands. After all, we are no longer under the law, right (Galatians 4:4-7)? However, to fully embrace grace without the truth would be to dismiss the righteousness of God. It brings about a mentality that we can do whatever our flesh desires without divine consequence because we have been forgiven already. What is missed in this attitude, however, is the love relationship with the Savior who forgives. If I am more in love with the things my flesh desires than the God Who freed me, then there is a problem. Jesus said, "Whoever has my commandments and keeps them, he it is who loves me. And he who loves me will be loved by my Father, and I will love him and manifest myself to him" (John 14:21). Grace does not negate the righteous instructions of God on the believer. Grace changes the motivation of the believer. Obedience changes from an act of *obligation* with the aim of approval to an act of *gratitude* for approval that has already been received.

On the flip-side, those who go to the extreme of truth without grace become entrenched in performance-based spirituality. To fully embrace truth without the grace that God provides would be to dismiss the sacrifice of Jesus on the cross as insufficient. Folks on this extreme measure everything and everybody by whether conformity to the code is being met. These individuals, in their zeal for the law, forget the purpose of the law. They easily slip into confusing their man-made traditions with the law of God. They constantly judge others, including themselves, based on both God's law and manmade traditions. In contrast, one of the main criticisms against Jesus was that He hung out with sinners (Matthew 9:10-13; 11:19). Jesus even got called a sinner for healing on the Sabbath (John 9:13-17). Jesus' own disciples got criticized for breaking the law by picking grain on the Sabbath and not ritually washing their hands (Luke 6:1-5; Mark 7:1-12). To both of these criticisms, Jesus threw the rebuke back at His accusers.

Grace and truth are not enemies. They are united. In Romans, Paul clearly states that grace is not a license to sin, but a motivator for righteous living (Romans 6). Because of grace, we are dead to sin. In Galatians, Paul does say, "But if you are led by the Spirit, you are not under the law" (Galatians 5:18). However, when you read the entire passage, he clearly makes a distinction between works of the Spirit and works of the flesh (Galatians 5:16-26). In boldly proclaiming that we are not under the law, Paul is still calling out sinful behavior.

The way Paul handles this concept in Colossians 2:16-3:15 nails down this balance. In the first half of that passage, he is dismissing legalism. Some of these restrictions were built upon Old Testament laws, some on man's traditions, and some on mystical religiosity. Folks were going around judging others by the standards of:

- what they ate, drank and touched (2:16, 21)
- when and how they worshipped (2:16-18)
- whether they had visions or if they followed others' visions (2:18)

To all of these, Paul is crystal clear: you are not bound in obligation to things such as this. All manners and expressions of religiousness are a shadow, but the true value belongs to Christ. Seeking after the elements to grow spiritually will never be sufficient, for true spiritual growth is found in what God is doing in us not what we are doing for him. He says in verse 20 that we have died to these oppressive regulations.

Given Paul's "freedom manifesto" here, one could walk away thinking that there are no relevant restrictions, commandments, or boundaries for the believer. Freedom is freedom and anything goes because it all is covered by grace.

However, the passage does not stop there. Immediately after Paul pronounces this freedom from regulations, he proclaims the vices that are not representative of a life that has been freed. Take a look at all of the acts of unrighteousness that Paul states we must put to death:

- Sexual immorality (3:5)
- Impurity (3:5)
- Passion (3:5)
- Evil Desire (3:5)
- Covetousness, which is idolatry ((3:5)
- Anger (3:8)
- Malice (3:8)
- Slander (3:8)
- Obscene Talk (3:8)
- Lying (3:9)

That is quite the list of offenses that Paul says should not be evident in the lives of those who love the Lord. So, what is Paul doing here? In one breath he is stating that we are not bound by regulations, human or otherwise, and in the other breath he is calling believers to stop committing these sins. Has Paul gone schizophrenic in a matter of minutes? Of course not.

The key to all of this is found right in the middle of the passage:

> "If then you have been raised with Christ, *seek* the things that are above, where Christ is, seated at the right hand of God. *Set your minds* on things that are above, not on things that are on earth. For you have died, and your life is hidden with Christ in God. *When Christ who is your life appears, then you also will appear with him in glory.*" (Colossians 3:1-4 *italics mine*)

Do you see it? The key to living in grace and truth is where we put our eyes. It's not about regulations, but it is also not about lawlessness. *It is all about Jesus.* When I put my faith in Jesus, He becomes my life. There will come a time when Jesus, my life, will return and take me with Him. Everything this world has to offer will one day pass away; therefore, it is all inferior to my relationship with Christ, which is eternal. I'm not bound by temporary obligations, but I am also not a slave to temporary indulgences. Everything I do or don't do in this temporary life must be filtered through the perspective of eternity.

My call is to be like Jesus until He returns. He never winked, dismissed, or laughed at sin. He also was the kind of person that sinners loved to hang around. He exuded truth and grace in a beautiful combination.

Brace the core and find the center of your balance. Embrace the core and find the freedom of living in grace and truth. "And whatever you do, in word or deed, do everything in the name of the Lord Jesus, giving thanks to God the Father through him" (Colossians 3:17).

CHAPTER 15

PRESSING ON

N O ONE WOULD LOOK AT ME AND THINK: "NOW there is a runner!" I am not a runner and would never claim to be, but I have ran before, believe it or not. I had a friend who tried to get me involved in a local "couch to 5k" group. I told him that was not my "thing." He said, "Well, you know, there are a lot of folks in this group who are not Christians and do not go to church." That was sneaky and manipulative! I was obligated to join now. I did the program and ran the 5k. It took everything within me and a lot of encouragement from others, but I endured. I finally tasted the satisfaction of simply crossing that finish line.

Paul talks about life as a race. The course of the race leads to the reward and no athlete runs except for the sole purpose of winning (1 Corinthians 9:24). Now, I am fully aware that at the local 5k level or even the big city marathon it is more about completing the race, not who wins or loses. But Paul is not writing about participation awards or even that we are racing against other runners. He is using the analogy of athletic competitions to bring home a relevant, spiritual truth. As believers, we have begun a race. It is a race that has a reward at the end for those who faithfully complete it. It is a race where our greatest adversary is ourselves. To run this race successfully will take everything we have.

How can we run this race in such a way as to win the prize? Every legit runner knows that smart running involves more than just strapping on an old pair of shoes and heading out. You need to make sure you have the right equipment. When I was in the process of going from couch to 5k, that same friend offered to buy me a really good pair of running shoes. I did not think I needed them, but man, what a difference they made. Good shoes, water bottle, rain gear, etc. These are simple, vital items one needs to accomplish that goal.

Look at what Paul has to say in Philippians 3:12-16:

> **12** Not that I have already obtained this or am already perfect, but I press on to make it my own, because Christ Jesus has made me his own. **13** Brothers, I do not consider that I have made it my own. But one thing I do: forgetting what lies behind and straining forward to what lies ahead, **14** I press on toward the goal for the prize of the upward call of God in Christ Jesus. **15** Let those of us who are mature think this way, and if in anything you think otherwise, God will reveal that also to you. **16** Only let us hold true to what we have attained.

In this passage, Paul lays out for us five essential elements that must be part of our running.

Dissatisfaction

First, Paul had a level of dissatisfaction with what he had accomplished in life. He states in verses 12 and 13 that he had not obtained [the prize] or been perfect or that he had made it on his own. His past was an essential part of his faith journey, but he could rest in his accomplishments. This does not mean that He was not content or satisfied in Christ. After all, shortly after he writes these words, he goes on to say that he has learned to be content in all circumstances (Philippians 4:11). He is content in Christ, but he is not satisfied with where he is on the journey. There is more to this race ahead.

When I ran that 5k, I could have easily gotten discouraged by those who were passing me. I could have also gotten an elevated view of myself based on the ones that I passed. I'm not lying—I did pass some folks! But the key to completing this race was not to compare myself to others; nor was it stopping at the 1k mark and calling it a day. It was evaluating myself based on my abilities and skill and pushing forward without giving up.

In the spiritual race, there will always be those who surpass us in spiritual aptitude, knowledge, or piety. There will also be those whom we pass. We are all at different places on the spectrum of spiritual growth. The key is to run *our own* race with faithfulness according to how God has gifted us. Proper self-evaluation keeps Jesus as the standard by which we measure and the hope for when we desperately fall short of that standard.

Focus

In verse 13, Paul states, "But one thing I do." One thing. This brings to mind a singular focus. There are many elements and obstacles that can impede our performance in the race; however, the secret to successful progress is to concentrate on one thing. Hebrews 12:1-2 echoes this sentiment:

> 1 Therefore, since we are surrounded by so great a cloud of witnesses, let us also lay aside every weight, and sin which clings so closely, and let us run with endurance the race that is set before us, 2 looking to Jesus, the founder and perfecter of our faith, who

for the joy that was set before him endured the cross,
despising the shame, and is seated at the right hand of
the throne of God.

Block out the noise of the crowd. Mute the screams as the body begs for relief. Maintain focus through all of the visual displays that vie for your attention.

No athlete succeeds by doing many things; rather, he specializes. Growing up, I loved to watch the decathlon at the Olympics. These were amazing athletes who would participate in 10 different track and field events: long jump, pole vaulting, shot put, running, etc. Their skills were phenomenal. Here's the catch, though: to be good at all 10 events meant that the athlete could not be the best at any individual event. If those decathletes were to compete in any one of those 10 events in an individual competition, they would most likely not place. Those who only commit to one sporting event generally are more competent in that one event than those who compete in many events. The reason for this is simple. The "one-event athletes" are able to devote themselves to only that event.

To run the spiritual race victoriously, you must be committed to that "one thing" above all. Everything else will fall into place after that, but nothing will succeed unless Jesus is first (John 6:33).

Direction

In verse 13, Paul states: "forgetting what lies behind and straining forward to what lies ahead." To forget does not mean that we fail to remember, it means that we will no longer be held back by what is in the past. Paul readily acknowledged his past, but only as a platform upon which to proclaim the transforming power of the gospel. Often, in salvation testimonies, much time is spent on how bad the person was in the past. This part of a testimony is important for context, but it is merely the setup. It all pales in comparison to the power of the gospel to transform that life. It all takes a backseat to the precious Savior who pulled the person out of the muck and the mire.

In addition, I often hear believers regretting the past. I totally understand that. Who would not want to go back and change some things? However, the Christian life is not dominated by what could have been. It is consumed by what Christ has done for us and where He is leading us. Therefore, we let go of those things from the past, our hurts, failures, abuses, etc., and cling to that which is before us: eternal resurrection. The race to the prize set before us must be run forward not in reverse.

Determination

Verse 14 reveals a powerful statement of determination. "I press on toward the goal for the prize of the upward call of God in Christ Jesus." Paul is indicating that he is pursuing this goal with full focus. What is the prize? If you look back at verse 12, he uses the same word. "I press on to make it my own." Make what his own? In the preceding verses he talks about the power of the resurrection and the fellowship in the sufferings of Christ. Therefore, the "upward call of God in Christ Jesus" in verse 14 is pointing back to the resurrection, which is preceded by the sufferings of Jesus. That is what Paul is pressing toward. His eyes, as he is running, are firmly focused on his ultimate resurrection, which is the prize! In this, he knows full well that suffering is a part of the path ahead, but he can gladly embrace those as well, because the ultimate prize is worth all of the difficulties in the journey!

By no means will the journey be easy. Any athlete who finds preparation and practice times easy and struggle-free is probably not pushing themselves hard enough. The journey is tough. The Word promised it would be. We love to cling to God's promises of victory, but we tend to gloss over the promises of difficulty (John 16:33; 2 Timothy 3:12-14;

James 1:2-4). Yet, it is in those proving grounds of life's struggles that our faith is refined, and the prize takes on an even greater appreciation.

It takes an intense fortitude and focus but also dependence on God to endure the hardships of the race to win the prize. Avoid the extremes. Some folks put a lot of reliance on themselves to run victoriously. They do their best and give it their all, but they also realize they do not have all it takes to come out ahead. On the other extreme, there are those who leave it all in God's hands. They trust Him to the point that they do not do anything. Eventually, they come to realize that they are not getting anywhere.

The biblically balanced perspective is that it is God who strengthens me to complete the race He set before me. I must run. He's not going to do that for me. However, I am incapable of completing that race on my own. This is the beauty of how God has chosen to work. He calls us to do more than we can do without His strength. It is a dependent—but not inactive—relationship. I must be determined to press on *in His power*.

Accountability (15-16)

I really like the way Paul sums up this section in verses 15 and 16. "Let those of us who are mature think this way, and if in anything you think otherwise, God will reveal that also to you. Only let us hold true to what we have attained." Paul recognized that his readers would be at different places and competencies in the spiritual journey. They certainly had not all endured all he had endured, or seen all he had seen. He knew that the same God who had embedded these truths on his heart would do the same for them in time. But the key was the forward movement in Christ. Pursue the Lord and press on for the prize in life. Hold fast to truth.

We have a tendency to think that spiritual maturity should be exhibited in every believer from the moment they put their faith in

Christ. We forget that when a person is born again that he is a baby in Christ. Growth is essential but it takes time. You can't feed a baby a steak. You can't make an overweight pastor, who doesn't run, complete a marathon. Training, learning, growing, and discipline are all part of the journey. We all are at different levels on the spiritual scale and different points on the spiritual spectrum; however, the key is that the believer is moving forward. We hold each other accountable for direction, not perfection.

One of the islands Tiffany and I visited on our 25th anniversary cruise was Katakolon, otherwise known as Ancient Olympia. It was the site of the first Greek games from around the 8th century BC. We saw ruins from those games. There was nothing like standing in that historic spot! We learned from our guide that the Greek games were very strict in obedience to rules. Similar to our modern Olympics, Greek athletes who disobeyed the rules would lose the right to compete for the prize. However, the ultimate accountability was not based on the athlete's ability, the popular opinion of the spectators, or even the esteem of their teammates. The final determination of whether an athlete was eligible, according to the rules, to compete for the prize was left solely to the judge(s) of the competition.

You and I are each running our races. We are competing against ourselves. Let us run in such a way that glorifies the Judge by keeping focused on the prize ahead.

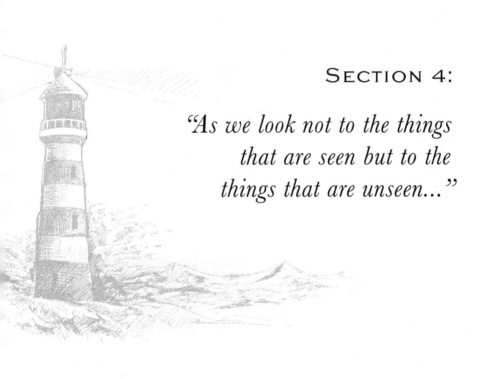

Section 4:

"As we look not to the things that are seen but to the things that are unseen..."

CHAPTER 16

THE JERK PRAYER

I LOVE MY LIFE GROUP! "LIFE GROUPS" IS THE NAME
we give our weekly small groups at my church. We get together
once a week, hashing out the practical applications of the sermon as
we fellowship and eat. It is a great place to be real and authentic in a
safe community.

One particular day, we began discussing our challenge to love
others when the "others" are jerks. I believe the question was: "But
there is this one person that, no matter how hard I try, I just can't seem
to love. What do I do?" I love this kind of honest transparency and I
think God does too!

You probably are experientially aware of the characteristics of these
kind of individuals this person was referring to. Jerks are typically the
kind of people who:

- Get under our skin
- Gossip
- Attack
- Bully
- Abuse
- Treat us unfairly
- Accuse

You know the type, right? Life on this earth will never be free from the jerks. After all, we only get 3 chapters into the Bible before the biggest jerk of all makes an appearance. Jerks stretch us to our limits.

It's easy to love the lovable...those folks who:

- Give you a good feeling
- Are Trustworthy
- Defend
- Build and encourage
- Protect
- Are fair and decent

It doesn't take faith or super spirituality to love those kinds of individuals. Literally, everyone can do that. Note what Jesus says:

> *"If you love those who love you, what benefit is that to you? For even sinners love those who love them. And if you do good to those who do good to you, what benefit is that to you? For even sinners do the same. And if you lend to those from whom you expect to receive, what credit is that to you? Even sinners lend to sinners, to get back the same amount. But love your enemies, and do good, and lend, expecting nothing in return, and your reward will be great, and you will be sons of the Most High, for he is kind to the ungrateful and the evil. Be merciful, even as your Father is merciful."* –Luke 6:32-36

It's simple human nature to love the lovable. Even those who are completely bound up in their sins are still willing to love, do good, and lend...at least to those who will ultimately provide benefit to them. On the other hand, it takes a super-nature to love those who hate you, do good to those who do bad to you, and lend to those who can give nothing in return.

Please understand that Jesus not only taught this concept, but He actually lived it. This was not simply philosophical and theoretical jargon, but impractical and unattainable! To the contrary, this concept was truth taught not only through words but in actions. As believers in Jesus, we understand this is the way things should be. We acknowledge this type of demeanor separates us from those without faith.

However, "understanding" and "acknowledging" refer to our mental and intellectual acceptance of truth. It takes us to another level of spiritual maturity when we actually attempt to put knowledge into action.

I remember when my son, Austin, was in those difficult middle school years. He always took words very seriously. Therefore, it wasn't hard to for the "bad guys" to discover my "Super-Son's" kryptonite: *words*. Kids would say stupid things to get under his skin, and inevitably his emotions would flare. He was never violent, but those words would cut deep and send him into an inconsolable zone. We spent many hours working on how to deal with jerks by continually reminding him that he was responsible for his actions and they were responsible for their actions, and that the words of the ignorant really should make no difference in our lives. We challenged him to respond to jerks with kindness and then walk away while shaking their nasty words off of his shoes. He knew that was true. He believed it. But putting it into practice proved to be incredibly challenging.

I am so grateful to be past those middle school years. However, jerks haven't ceased to exist. Our lives are full of them and dealing with them is still quite a challenge.

I am amazed by the words and actions of Jesus. Look again at what He said at the end of Luke 6:35b: *"And you will be sons of the Most High, for he is kind to the ungrateful and the evil."* These words stop me in my tracks. Think about it. I'm to do these difficult tasks because God is kind to the ungrateful and the evil?! Why in heaven's name is God being kind to the ungrateful and the evil? Why is He not destroying them immediately? Then the truth bowls me over like a wrecking ball: I'm the one receiving His kindness. I was the ungrateful and evil one. His kindness of salvation was offered to me when I was unworthy. I'm no longer part of that group of evil; I'm now a son of the Most High. However, with my new designation comes a responsibility to show that kindness and mercy to those for whom He died. He loves, therefore I love. He does good, therefore I do good. He gave freely, therefore I give freely. As a believer, having received tons of mercy and grace and the power of the Holy Spirit, my calling is to give those things to others, whether they receive it or not.

So, how can we embrace this practically when faced with the ungratefulness and evilness of jerks? There are many things I could suggest, but at the top of the list is: Pray for the jerks in your life. It sure is easy to say, "Pray about it." It's quite another to actually deliver on that intent. So, in Life Group that night, I suggested that when they didn't have the words to say, they could pray the Word of God back to Him. Let our words be conformed to His words. When you try this, flip some of the words around so that it becomes personal communication to God.

The first passage that came to mind was Romans 12:9-21. This has always been my first "go-to" passage when helping people deal with jerks in their lives. I decided to make it a prayer for this discussion. I would encourage you to read the passage of Scripture first in your Bible. Then read the prayer I constructed from it. This is just my way of wording it. Really everyone's prayer should be different. Same Word but different prayers back to God through our unique perspectives, backgrounds, and circumstances. Do it your way...just you and God.

My friend Kirby titled this the "Jerk Prayer." Love it! Embrace it! Use it!

The Jerk Prayer (Romans 12:9-21)

Lord, You know how hard it is for me to love *{Insert the name of someone you are having a tough time loving}*. I need Your help.

9 Help me love *{Same individual}* with genuineness. I want the only hate I have to be for what is evil, which includes the bitterness I sometimes harbor. I truly desire to hold tightly to what is good.

10 Help me to love others with brotherly affection, a love based on intrinsic human worth and not performance. I don't want anyone to outdo me showing honor to others.

11 Help me to resist laziness when it comes to serving You, Lord; rather, I want to go all out in serving You, full of energy, with a passion and zeal in my spirit, realizing that my service to others is really my service to You.

12 Help me change my *perspective*: rejoicing in hope. Help me change my *demeanor*: being patient in tribulation. Help me change my *posture*: being constant in prayer. **13** Use me to help meet the needs of Your children. Build within me the yearning to show hospitality.

14 I ask You to bless those who persecute me. Help me to be a blessing to them. Help me to speak kindly to them and about them.

15 I want to join with others in their triumphs and tragedies. Help me rejoice with those who rejoice and in no way be jealous. Help me weep with those who weep and not be apathetic.

16 I desire, Lord, to live in harmony with others. Convict and correct me if I have a prideful attitude or neglect others for prejudicial reasons.

I know that I am nothing apart from You and that wisdom and discernment come from You alone.

17 Help me to be *proactive*, doing what is honorable and right in Your eyes, and not *reactive*, responding to evil with unrighteous thoughts or actions.

18 I know, Lord, that I alone am responsible for my actions and others will answer for theirs. I make a commitment to do everything I can, within my means, to live at peace with others, but I will leave the results up to You.

19 Lord, I will not seek revenge on those who have hurt me; rather, I will trust You to handle that business in Your own way. Your wrath will always accomplish more than my little efforts could anyway. After all, You said, "Vengeance is mine, I will repay."

20 I am trusting You for that, I am totally free now to feed my hungry enemy and if he is thirsty, then I will give him a drink. Ironically, when I go the extra mile for him in Your name, then all of the blame begins to shift to him, the results of which can be awfully painful. I'd much rather be on the side of righteousness and mercy than the side that rakes in the judgment.

21 Help me, Lord, to live as the overcomer I am in You and not fall into the trap of defeat and regret resulting from giving in to evil.

CHAPTER 17

REEVALUATING THE UNDERDOG
(Pt. 1–Recognizing Identity)

THERE IS SOMETHING ABOUT THE STORY OF THE underdog that compels us. The Rocky movies would have never had such an appeal if he was expected to prevail. Whether it was against Creed, Mr. T, or the huge Russian, it was always a journey against all odds. Even when he was the champ, the brutal nature and imposing disposition of his opponents made conventional wisdom view him as an underdog. One of my favorite sequences in all the series was in Rocky IV when Rocky is training to fight the Russian who killed his once rival but eventual friend, Apollo Creed. While his opponent is in the finest facilities with top-of-the-line equipment, Rocky is training in the blistering cold of the Russian countryside with common farm tools. Everything was stacked against him, but, of course, the glory comes in the end when he defeats the Russian on his own turf. Watching that victory made me want to jump up, fists to the sky!

We have encountered many such stories in real life and they all amaze and inspire us. A composer who is deaf creates a masterpiece. A gymnast with a bum ankle nails the final vault to capture gold. The U.S. Olympic hockey team defies the odds and beats the powerhouse

Russian team. A pitcher with one arm makes the major leagues. We love the stories of the underdog. We aren't the only ones though.

Could it be that the soft spot for the underdog is not simply a human emotion, but a part of the image God instilled in us? God loves the underdog. We see it time and time again throughout the Bible. A man with a speech impediment stands before the dictator of an oppressive nation and demands that he release all the country's slave labor. A young teenager faces a giant opponent while the entire army of his home nation trembles in fear. An unwed teenager becomes the chosen woman to bring forth the long-awaited savior. A fast-talking, quick-tempered fisherman becomes a preacher of humility, gentleness, and righteousness in the midst of suffering for following Christ. The chief persecuting pawn of the religious legalists becomes a mouthpiece for the gospel of grace throughout the world.

The underdog is in the perfect position to put the glory of God on display. It is in the midst of unconquerable enemies, when we are stripped down to nothing but undeniable weakness, that God's power comes through. It's not just that we find ourselves in these positions; rather, it is often true that God *chooses* to put us in these positions. Sometimes, we are too quick to trust in our own sufficiency. We think we got it covered, figured out, down pat, or solved—but we don't. Other times, we cower at our circumstances. We think we are inadequate, confused, or too scared, but we aren't. Through our limited, temporal perspective, we can often view our problems as too big or too small. How about viewing them like this: Our problems are big; our God is bigger. Hoping in ourselves will bring defeat; trusting in Him will bring victory.

I love the contrast in perspectives we see in the story of Gideon in Judges 6. The angel of the LORD shows up to Gideon during a season of defeat. Israel is under constant bullying by a neighboring nation called Midian. Every time Israel plants a crop or corrals livestock, Midian comes in and destroys everything. There is simply nothing that

Israel can do to stop it. Midian is the Russian boxer Drago looking down at Apollo saying, "If he dies, he dies." *Ugh!* Bullies are the worst!

So, Gideon is threshing wheat in the winepress. Why? A winepress is for grapes, not wheat. But Gideon is trying to hide the harvested crops from the bullies. In this moment, the angel of the LORD shows up at this clandestine winepress and makes 2 astonishing proclamations to Gideon: "The LORD is with you, O mighty man of valor...Go in this might of yours and save Israel from the hand of Midian" (Judges 6:12,14). What a way to start a conversation! Gideon is stunned in two major ways. First, this stranger sure did have a lot of nerve to say that God was with him. By all accounts, it seemed God had deserted Israel, leaving them to reap the consequences of their spiritual prostitution. They were on their own and barely surviving. (v.13) Secondly, "mighty man of valor" and "save Israel?" Gideon must have been sure this stranger had mistaken him for someone else. This stranger was deranged! Here he was, beating out wheat secretly, paranoid that some of those bullies would pounce on him and destroy his labor. Not only that, but he was also considered the least in his family—which was the weakest tribe. (v.15) In Gideon's mind, when it came to all of the men in Israel, he was the lowest man of all.

But alas, that is where the eternal perspective meets the temporal perspective. What you see is not always what you get. The eternal message from God was this: "I never left Israel, you left me. I have you, Israel, exactly where I want you, crying out for Me. And you are exactly the man I am looking for—weak and desperate." Gideon was blown away by what he was hearing, but he also was skeptical. He needed proof.

So, what did Gideon do? Well, of course, he made the stranger a meal. Isn't that what you would do when your mind has just been blown by such a confusing conversation? And what did the angel of the LORD do? Well, of course, he touched the meal with his staff and burned it all up. Makes perfect sense, right? What God declares; He means. He is not playing around. His declarations are like fire:

all-consuming. Gideon's response? "Now I understand who I am dealing with? This is no ordinary stranger. I just stood face to face with the angel of the LORD! I'm a dead man now" (v.22 *my paraphrase*) God reassures Gideon that He brings peace, not death. (v.23) Gideon immediately responds by building an altar to God and calls it "The LORD is Peace."

The next step was crucial for this underdog. God tells him to go and tear down the idols his father had built to the false gods Baal and Asherah. In their place, Gideon was to sacrifice two of his father's bulls to the one true God of Israel. Gideon obeys, but with fear. He is caught in the middle of opposing realities and he is having trouble reconciling the two. He is convinced that he has met with the LORD. He is also convinced that if and when his family finds out about his desecration of the false god altars, they will have his head. So, he follows God's command, but does it at night to avoid scrutiny.

Have you realized yet, in this story, that you are an underdog as well? This is Gideon's story, but the implications have application for all of us. Many times, we find ourselves in the middle of those contrasting realities. On one side, we have the world telling us what we can and can't do. Society declares who we are, dictates what acceptable behavior should be, and shoves it in our faces. On the other side, God is telling us who we are in His eyes, and based on that truth, what our lives should look like. These two realities are diametrically opposed. We can't just set our altar to God beside the altar to Baal and try to find the balance. No. One of them must come down for the other to be built.

The believer in Jesus Christ is perceived in different ways. He is an underdog in the minds of the world versus a victorious warrior in the mind of God. But God puts a condition on this warrior status. It's not that he must be the strongest, the bravest, the smartest, or the wealthiest. The condition is that he has to stake his allegiance to the one true God and that stance will cost him. Just as Gideon had to tear down the altars, so must we. Just as Gideon had to risk his reputation and inheritance and even his life, so must we. There was no other way for Gideon to live out his God-given identity. We are the same; victory can only begin with surrender.

So, Gideon obeys God and, sure enough, people in his tribe come for his head. When the men in town rose early, they immediately found the Baal altar and Asherah pole torn down (v. 28). This tells us how much this idolatry was a part of the regular routine of their lives. Like an addict who needs drugs, not to feel high but to feel normal, this worship of false gods was their safe and beloved normal. But this addictive lie had been torn down and they were livid. They were on the warpath after Gideon.

This conflict put Gideon's dad, Joash, in a pickle. He was the one who had erected the altars to the false gods. He was also loved his son. In that moment, he found a way out. He stated to the mob: "Will you contend for Baal? Or will you save him? Whoever contends for him shall be put to death by morning. If he is a god, let him contend for himself, because his altar has been broken down." (v. 31) Basically, if Baal is who you believe him to be, then let him kill Gideon; however, if you have to do it for him, then maybe you should be the one on the chopping block. Statements like that remind me of those choice questions we see many times in the Bible which stop people in their tracks. Jesus tells the religious leaders to go ahead and let the stones fly as soon as they can confidently claim perfection in their own lives. (John 8:7) Gamaliel challenges the Jewish council to hold off on killing the disciples because if the gospel they proclaim was not from God, then it would die out eventually; however, if it perseveres, then did they really want the blood of the God-sent on their hands? (Acts 5:34-40)

Looking at ourselves and our circumstances through an eternal perspective requires a few adjustments to our perception. First, we actually have to embrace the role of the underdog in our own strength. Gideon had no trouble with this aspect. Rocky did. It was those times when Rocky was the champ and the favorite that he got sloppy. Then he would get defeated. True victory for the believer comes when we first recognize that on our own, we are nothing.

Secondly, we must believe that we are who God says we are. The value that the world places on us is built on the temporal and self-serving desires from the flesh. The value that God places on us is built on the eternal glory of God. Check out 1 Peter 2:9-10 and feast on this truth:

> *9 But you are a chosen race, a royal priesthood, a holy nation, a people for his own possession, that you may proclaim the excellencies of him who called you out of darkness into his marvelous light. 10 Once you were not a people, but now you are God's people; once you had not received mercy, but now you have received mercy.*

Thirdly, we must embrace our new identity in the Lord which makes a direct impact on how we live our lives. Being in Christ changes everything. If the believer's identity is spelled out in 1 Peter 2:9-10, then the implications of that identity are elaborated in verses 11-12:

> *11 Beloved, I urge you as sojourners and exiles to abstain from the passions of the flesh, which wage war against your soul. 12 Keep your conduct among the Gentiles honorable, so that when they speak against you as evildoers, they may see your good deeds and glorify God on the day of visitation.*

There are worse things than being considered the underdog. In fact, that position is right where God wants us so that His glory can be on display.

CHAPTER 18

REEVALUATING THE UNDERDOG

(Pt. 2–Embracing Victory)

A FTER A WEEK AND HALF OF MISSION AND MINISTRY work in Brazil, it was time to take a day to do something fun before heading home. It was suggested that we go paragliding. I was unsure about it, but it looked pretty cool. As we hiked up the mountain, I made a deal with William Wilson that he would go first so I could see how it all went. After all, I was the one with a fear of heights. We finally reached a fairly large field about halfway up the mountain that provided an overlook of the valley below. As we stepped up onto the field from the trail, we witnessed several paragliders swooping here and there overhead. Honestly, my knees began to quiver just looking up at them. I remember looking at William and saying, "Man...I don't know." He laughed and said something about it being all good. His words were a little mumbled in my head as I was trying to figure out an escape plan. At least he was going to go first and that would buy me time—or so I thought.

The next few moments were a bit of a whirlwind in my memory. These guys started putting the harness on me amid my calls for them to stop and directing them toward Wilson, who was supposed to go first. None of my pleas for sanity worked and these Portuguese-speaking kidnappers remained diligent in their task of strapping me up for the death flight. Another guy, who I had actually paid to take a video of the experience, was now shoving a camera in my face for a reaction. I tried my best to hold it together, but my anxiety was creeping out behind that forced smile.

They then strapped me to my guide who was connected to the parachute. Within a matter of seconds, the parachute caught air. This is the point at which you are supposed to run forward off of the mountain. *Nope! I'm not insane. Not going to happen.* I went ahead and sat down in the little nylon seat. The unsympathetic dude, strapped to my back, was telling me to get up so he could more easily walk us off of the cliff. *Sorry bro. You are on your own.* He mustered all of his strength, pushing through my enormous dead weight, and ran full force, straight ahead, into a place where logic says you should never go. Our feet left the secure ground, and we were airborne. I was gripping the straps so tight that my knuckles were turning white, embracing the fantasy that holding onto this flying device brought me any security. We soared up to 3,000 feet above the mountain. It was the perfect combinations of:

> fear and exhilaration,
> anxiety and trust,
> hanging on and letting go.

In many ways, it is a metaphor for life.

I imagine that Gideon had similar feelings as he faced insurmountable odds. He had been obedient to the LORD and torn down the altars to the false gods. He even got a new name out of the deal: Jerubbaal ("Let Baal contend against him." Judges 6:32). He also got a new "wardrobe." "But the Spirit of the LORD clothed Gideon" (6:34). The work had just begun.

The massive armies of the Midianites and the Amalekites were bearing down on these tribes from Israel. Gideon knew that God had called him to lead Israel in defeating them, but there were still seeds of doubt. These seeds of doubt are similar to the times we clearly know God is calling us to do something, but we are still inhibited by fear. Do we take a stand for integrity while everyone around us is compromising? Can we talk to someone about the gospel, when the Spirit prompts us, even though it is difficult to do so? Will we forgive, as He commands, or let bitterness be too great an obstacle to overcome? Do we ask forgiveness from someone we may have wronged, or let pride be the insurmountable barrier?

Gideon wanted confirmation before he laid everything on the line. So, he determined to put God to the test. He laid out a fleece of wool with *instructions* for God. "If there is dew on the fleece alone, and it is dry on all the ground, then I shall know that you will save Israel by my hand, as you have said" (Judges 6:37).

Now, let's take a short breather here. Giving God instructions is never the best tactic. The whole potter and clay thing comes into play here (Isaiah 29:16; 64:8; Jeremiah 18:1-10; Romans 9:21). In addition, Gideon was basically saying, "I know you have told me to do this, but I just have to be sure."

If I were God, I would have said something like, "Did I stutter? Get to it boy!" But God was—and is—gracious and patient in our times of doubt.

Gideon woke up the next morning and God delivered on the sign. The fleece was wet, and the ground was dry. "Well," Gideon must have thought, "maybe one more time for good measure." This time Gideon reverses it and God comes through again: dry fleece, wet ground. God is not obligated to always give repetitive confirmations like a parent who should only have to issue an instruction once. Even more so, God should only have to say things once. Gratefully, though, He is faithful even when our faith is struggling.

With the fleece confirmation given, Gideon began to assemble his small army. He was able to recruit around 32,000 people to battle against a Midianite and Amalekite army of about 135,000. God looked at the assembled army and immediately said that there are too many soldiers. He issued a reprieve for all the soldiers who were afraid of going into battle. At that call, 22,000 troops returned home leaving 10,000 remaining troops. There were still too many. The next time, God used a water test. He told Gideon to separate the ones who lapped up the water with their tongues like a dog and sent them home. That left 300 men, the ones who knelt down and drug the water hand-to-mouth, ready for battle. The odds were established: 135,000 enemy soldiers versus 300 men and one big God.

God, ever-loving and patient with His young leader, gave Gideon another confirmation. He told Gideon that if he was still scared, to head on down to the enemy camp on a recon mission. Gideon snuck up to the edge of camp and listened in as an enemy soldier recounted a dream he had. In this dream, a "cake of barley bread tumbled into the camp of Midian and came to the tent and struck it so that it fell and turned it upside down, so that the tent lay flat" (Judges 7:13). Immediately, one of his fellow soldiers interpreted the dream to be about Gideon (the loaf of barley bread) and the fall of Midian (the tent). The Midianite army (tent) was massive, more camels than one could count, and they made a habit of coming in and devouring the land like locusts (Judges 6:5). This massive army was to be put down by a loaf of barley, the poor man's bread.[12] Empowered with this confirmation, Gideon headed back to his camp to get his army.

Isn't it amazing how God is so gracious? Think about it. He knows the end from the beginning. Nothing surprises Him or catches Him off guard. He is intimately involved in the process. Note how He had already given the dream to the Midianite soldier before Gideon ever secretly approached the camp. God is always at work, whether we see actual evidence of it or not. All we have to do is trust Him, keep the

---

[12] *Easton Bible Dictionary*, s.v. "barley," accessed April 25, 2020, http://eastonsbible-dictionary.org/451-Barley.php

faith, and press on. But when we stumble, doubt, or slow down, He is still right there with us. To Gideon's credit, at least to this point, he was always aware of his utter dependence on the Lord. His desire for confirmation seemed to be more about confidence that the Lord was with them rather than doubt that the Lord would come through.

As if the strange methods of confirmations and army reductions were not enough, the warfare strategy was absurd—to the natural mind. God led the 300 to set a perimeter about the enemy camp. Each man had 2 full hands. In one hand was a trumpet and in the other was a torch covered by a jar. When the time was right, they broke the jars revealing the torches and blew the trumpets and shouted, "A sword for the LORD and for Gideon!" (7:20). With the stillness of the night pierced by the amplified chorus and voices and trumpets and the darkness of night set ablaze, the confused Midianites stumbled out of bed and began to slash one another. "The LORD set every man's sword against his comrade and against all of the army. And the army fled" (7:22).

Amid overwhelming odds, victory was delivered to the Israelites. And during the chaos of battle, a hero emerged. From places unseen, unknown, and seemingly out of nowhere, a hero is recognized. His name and fame started to spread throughout humanity. The hero is not Gideon, mind you. The hero is the LORD!

Do you see God's hand in all of this? He is the One who called this weak man from a weak tribe of Israel to lead the people. He is the One who promised His presence. He is the One who patiently confirmed the calling. He is the One who stacked the odds in favor of the enemy. He is the One who set the whole thing up so that His people and other nations would know He is the One true God. Nobody else could have gotten the credit for this account.

The hero in your story is not you. The hero in my story is not me. We certainly have the tendency to buy into our own hype and believe that we are all we need. But God is continually setting us up to see our own inadequacies. He is determined to glorify Himself in our lives. Isn't that arrogant of God? No way! To be arrogant is to exaggerate one's own worth or importance.[13] Since God is the Creator of the universe and Author of all that is, there is no way to exaggerate Him at all. All things are under Him and belong to Him!

We get frustrated when we are at the end of our abilities, skills, energy, and strength, however, that is exactly where God wants us. We get discouraged when circumstances seemingly don't work out to our advantage, but God is still working in and through those circumstances. In these moments and so many more, God is developing our faith and showing off His strength, power, and purpose.

Gideon, like most of us, does not fit into simple categories that describe either unrighteousness or righteousness. He righteously tore down the idols and led Israel to defeat its foes and even made the proclamation: "I will not rule over you, and my son will not rule over you; the LORD will rule over you" (Judges 8:23). Yet, he also took a bunch of gold and made an ephod out of it, which the Israelites "whored after it there, and it became a snare to Gideon and to his family" (8:27). He struggled with women, having 70 sons from many wives and concubines (8:30-31). And after 40 years of peace, as soon as Gideon died, so did his legacy. The people immediately

> "turned again and whored after the Baals and made Baal-berith their god. And the people of Israel did not remember the LORD their God, who had delivered them from the hand of all their enemies on every side, and they did not show steadfast love to the family of Jerubbaal (that is, Gideon) in return for all the good that he had done to Israel" –Judges 8:33-35

---

[13] Webster's Dictionary, s.v. "arrogant," accessed April 25, 2020, https://www.merriam-webster.com/dictionary/arrogant

In Gideon's story, we see a human man brought up out of weakness and obscurity to lead a nation. He had doubt and faith, boldness and weakness, courage and blind spots, righteousness and unrighteousness. But most of all, he had the LORD. In the mixed bag of good and evil in our lives, may we fix our eyes on the truth that as believers in Jesus Christ, through it all, He is with us to glorify Himself. Surrender to Him. Trust in Him. Obey Him. Victory is around the corner.

CHAPTER 19

WHERE'S MY MIRACLE?

A DISEASED GALLBLADDER IS NO JOKE. AS A PASTOR, I have prayed for many different physical ailments, diseases, and struggles that my members have gone through. I've prayed for folks' gallbladder issues before, but this was my first personal experience with one. It began with chest pain on a Sunday morning. I was "forced" by my caring wife and the posse she rounded up to go to the ER. They saw something a little strange with my EKG and it was on. I was in the hospital for a couple of days being put through the ringer and then finally released after nothing showed up. By that, I mean nothing was wrong— my heart did show up. I *do* have a heart for any doubters out there.

As the week progressed, my discomfort increased. Saturday night, I could only sleep if a hot compress was on my abdomen. Once it cooled down, I woke back up in pain. Tiffany knew I was in bad shape when I was the one who said, "Back to the ER!" I was in such agony that I ended up laying on the floor—yeah, that's right—the floor of the ER's waiting room. *Nasty!* These were desperate times, though, and I needed relief. Once they got me back, an ultrasound revealed an enlarged gallbladder. It had to come out.

Because I had been in a week earlier with "heart" related issues, they required that the cardiologist sign off on my gallbladder surgery. I had to lay on my back in the hospital for 2 full days awaiting cardiac clearance for this surgery. Morphine was not eliminating this pain, only dulling it. It wasn't just the pain that was getting to me. Because they did not know when my surgery was going to be, I could not eat or drink anything. I could not even chew on an ice chip! The only thing they would let me have for 2 solid days was a moist sponge on a stick that I could rub on my lips.

Miserable!

But then the time came for the surgery. They put me to sleep to take out my "partially gangrenous" gallbladder from my navel. Yeah, you don't want to ever hear the word "gangrenous" about anything inside or outside of your body. When I came to, I was sitting up in bed in the recovery room. I looked down and in my hand was a Styrofoam cup full of that good ice, you know the kind that is small and soft? I quickly looked up at the nurse and said, "Can I eat this?"

She looked at me like I was crazy and said, "Sure." It was on like Donkey Kong! I tore into that ice. It was the sweetest tasting, most satisfying ice I have ever had! Sheer joy in a cup. Who would have thought?

When I think about my two days of torture, my mind starts to think about those accounts we read about in the Gospels about individuals who had major physical, spiritual, emotional, and mental issues before having miraculous encounters with the Savior. My issue only lasted a little over a week. Some of these folks had been dealing with difficulties their entire lives.

We find one such instance in John 5:1-17 where Jesus encounters a man who had been an invalid for 38 years. We do not know if this man was born lame, developed it or had an accident. We do know that for 38 years he had been unable to care for himself. When Jesus entered the pool called Bethesda, He was no doubt surrounded by many invalids; however, he focused on this one man. He asked him a question which most of us would have taken as rhetorical: "Do you want to be healed?" (John 5:6). I mean, who wouldn't want to be healed? Then again, when someone gets used to their state of suffering it can become all they know. As strange as it sounds, they can actually become so used to the daily routine of suffering that they are too comfortable to change. The man explains to Jesus that when the water is stirred, he can't make it to the water in time to get healed. Jesus then makes an amazing statement to this man: "Get up, take up your bed, and walk" (John 5:8).

Jesus healed the man, but he also gave him a responsibility. This wasn't a passive healing, there was action involved. He gave four commands to the man (three of them in verse 8 and then a fourth we will see later). These commands are applicable to us today as we seek to follow Christ with an eternal perspective.

Get up!

This man was lame for 38 years. He became a piece of the scenery at the pool called Bethesda. He was overlooked. People, no doubt, stepped over him and around him. But Jesus stopped, spoke, and healed. Now it was time for the man to get up. This was something he had not done in nearly 4 decades, no doubt his muscles were atrophied. This was new, but the time for lying down had come to an end. He would no longer be defined by his limitations. There was not another soul in the world who would have made such a bold command to this man, but Jesus did.

The world we live in will constantly attempt to define us by our attributes and/or our limitations. We are often assigned worldly value by our looks, our abilities, our wealth, our popularity or the lack of any of those temporal assets. But they don't get to define us because Christ already has. Don't let the perceptions, biases and preferences of the world keep you paralyzed. Get up and be who God created you to be.

Take up your bed!

The bed became a physical representation of the man's identity. It was one of his sole possessions and it was crucial to his life as a lame man; after all, he was confined to lying around day and night. Any movement from that mat had to be with the help of others. Now Jesus says, "Take up your bed." Why? He was to take up his bed because he no longer needed it. He could walk!

We are not simply to get up, we are to let go. As the man was to take up his bed as a symbol that he no longer needed it, so we should "take up" our old ways of life. We do not need them anymore. Just as the world no longer defines our value, neither do the things that represent our former lives. It doesn't mean that we should strip naked and live in the ditch. We can have things, but the difference is that things can no longer *have us*. This formerly lame man would most likely still sleep on a bed, but he no longer had to live on one. The bottle, the needle, the bank account, the fancy cars and houses, the athletic ability, and a myriad of other things that vie for our allegiance in this world no longer have a hold on us. They may serve a purpose, but they are no longer the purpose to be served.

Walk away!

Once he got up, he had to walk. He had to leave his home at the pool of Bethesda. He was literally walking away from his previous life. His former surroundings were suitable for his former life, but they were no longer adequate for a new life. The setting was designed for the reasonable comfort of an invalid, but it had no value for someone who could walk.

When we put our faith in Jesus Christ, the Bible says that we are born again. This imagery is repeated throughout Scripture. In having a new life in Christ, we have put to death the old life. We are not meant to return to the grave. The former places where we lived in comfort that massaged our flesh nature are no longer places in which we can hang out anymore.

Walk toward!

Jesus later encounters the man at the temple and gives him one more piece of instruction: "See, you are well! Sin no more, that nothing worse may happen to you" (John 5:14). What could possibly be "worse" for this man to encounter? Life apart from the Lord forever, that's what! Jesus was not telling the man that he had been lame due to his sin. The "sin no more" was a call to repentance which insinuated a call to faith in the One who had healed him. What good would it do ultimately if the man could walk this earth but ultimately spend eternity condemned?

The call to walk away from our dead life in sin is coupled with a call to walk toward a new life in Christ. The charge to "sin no more" was not intended as an unrealistic call to sinless perfection. It had more to do with turning from sin and viewing it the way our Savior does. We may be unable to completely eliminate sin as long as we are in these fallen bodies, however, our posture has changed. We hate sin and we pursue righteousness in the Lord. It is not about perfection; it is about direction.

Now some will read all of this and say, "Yeah, yeah, I hear you. I have been trying to do all of that, but I am still struggling with a need here. I still need a miracle. I'm praying and nothing is happening. Where is my miracle?" I hear the heart and struggle in these words. Whether it is for personal healing or the healing of a loved one, we cry out for God's intervention. We read stories of miracles and wonder why we are not experiencing the same thing in our own lives.

I want you to read what I am about to write through the lens of compassion. Here is the truth: It's not your miracle. This miracle did not belong to the lame man. In other parts of Scripture, we find Jesus healing a woman with a blood issue, a blind man, a demon-possessed man, and even a dead man. None of these miracles were primarily for the recipients. That may seem crazy at first glance, but it is true. None of those miracles were for the people who benefited from them. All of those miracles were about Jesus. The main person in all miracles is the Healer, not the one being healed.

The end of this passage says, "And this was why the Jews were persecuting Jesus, because he was doing these things on the Sabbath. But Jesus answered them, 'My Father is working until now, and I am working'" (John 5:16-17). John is clearly telling the reader why he included this account. This healing was about Jesus and showing why the Jewish leaders persecuted him for it.

God elevates His glory above our personal needs. Again, I know this may sound like a crazy concept, but it is true. Ultimately, God is glorified in sending His Son to die on our behalf for our sins which we could not atone for ourselves. He is glorified in the resurrection of Jesus Christ, conquering death and hell for us. He is glorified in ascending to heaven, preparing a place for us, and sending the Holy Spirit to indwell believers. He is glorified and one day, He will return and clothe us with glorified bodies. He will welcome us into the eternal kingdom with Him where everything is set right.

Therefore, when God is glorified, we ultimately become the recipients of the greatest blessings. Whether we experience healing in the here and now or not, His glory is more important than our comfort. When He does choose to heal, it is about exalting Himself. When He does not choose to heal, it is still about exalting Himself. We can take confidence in the fact that everything in our lives, the good and the bad, the wanted and the unwanted, the answered prayers and the "unanswered" prayers, the pain and wellness, are all working together for His glory and our good.

Get up! Take up your bed! Walk! Go sin no more!

CHAPTER 20

DUMB IDOLS

I HAD ONE DAY OFF OUT OF 14 ON THAT FIRST mission trip to Vietnam. My translator wanted to take me to a popular tourist destination called the Marble Mountains outside of Hoi An. As we hiked up the trails and steps and ventured into the man-carved caves, we witnessed many statues dedicated to deities within Buddhist and Hinduist religious traditions. I stood side by side with one of the Buddha statues and stuck my belly out *(didn't have to work too hard at that!)* and took a picture. I don't get people sometimes. Just because I'm bald and have a big belly does not mean I look like Buddha! Come on folks, I don't wear a robe out in public. Enough said.

So, as we made our way from one cave sanctuary to another, I was amazed by the number of people who were bowing down and praying to these statues. I had the same feeling when, in the lobby of the hotels I stayed in, they would often have a little shrine to Buddha or other gods. They would have fresh fruit before the gods and light incense. The fragrant smell was usually too much for my sensitive olfactory nerves.

Here is the thing. Those statues were carved by human hands. They did not spontaneously come into existence, nor were they eternal. They were made with the elements that come out of the earth and formed by human beings. Ironically, the creators were worshipping the created.

In Exodus 20:3-6, we have the account of God giving Moses the 10 commandments for His people. He began the list like this:

> *You shall have no other gods before me. You shall not make for yourself a carved image, or any likeness of anything that is in heaven above, or that is in the earth beneath, or that is in the water under the earth. You shall not bow down to them or serve them, for I the Lord your God am a jealous God, visiting the iniquity of the fathers on the children to the third and the fourth generation of those who hate me, but showing steadfast love to thousands of those who love me and keep my commandments.*

This instruction was built upon verse 2 which was the foundational principle that "I am the LORD your God."

God makes it clear that man was to reject idols. While God was giving Moses instructions up on the mountain, take a wild guess what the people were doing in the valley below. They were pushing Aaron to make a statue for them to worship. You see, they felt like they had to see something to be able to worship God. When Moses came down off of the mountain with the tablets, written on by God Himself, it all broke loose.

This idolatry was a continual struggle through Israel's history. If our understanding is that idols are simply statues or graven images, chances are that you might not struggle in this area. My guess is that you do not have a room in your house dedicated to an idol or idols. But are we right to limit idolatry to simply the graven image?

Martin Luther is quoted as saying, "Anything that one imagines of God apart from Christ is only useless thinking and vain idolatry... Not only the adoration of images is idolatry, but also trust in one's own righteousness, works and merits, and putting confidence in riches and power. As the latter is the commonest, so it also is the most noxious."[14]

You see, idolatry is not some ancient problem limited to the Israelites and their pagan neighbors. Nor is it only an issue represented in eastern mysticism or religions. It is an ever-present temptation for all of us.

I recently came across this passage in Isaiah that just kept jumping off the page at me. I spent much time over the course of a year returning to and meditating on this passage. It spoke volumes to me, not just in the context of Israel's judgement, but in our lives today.

In the first part of Isaiah, we see God speaking through the prophet casting judgement on them. This judgement was going to come through Babylon. Captivity was on the way. But the rest of Isaiah proclaims God's sovereignty and how God was going to bring them back. In the midst of this, we get this astounding proclamation in Isaiah 46.

1 Bel bows down; Nebo stoops; their idols are on beasts and livestock. these things you carry are borne as burdens on weary beasts.
2 They stoop; they bow down together; they cannot save the burden, but themselves go into captivity.
3 "Listen to me, O house of Jacob, all the remnant of the house of Israel, who have been borne by me from before your birth, carried from the womb;
4 even to your old age I am he, and to gray hairs I will carry you. I have made, and I will bear; I will carry and will save.
5 "To whom will you liken me and make me equal, and compare me, that we may be alike?
6 Those who lavish gold from the purse, and weigh out silver in the scales,

---

[14] https://www.azquotes.com/author/9142-Martin_Luther/tag/idolatry, accessed April 26, 2020.

hire a goldsmith, and he makes it into a god; then they fall down and worship!

7 They lift it to their shoulders, they carry it, they set it in its place, and it stands there; it cannot move from its place. If one cries to it, it does not answer or save him from his trouble.

8 "Remember this and stand firm, recall it to mind, you transgressors, 9 remember the former things of old; for I am God, and there is no other; I am God, and there is none like me,

10 declaring the end from the beginning and from ancient times things not yet done, saying, 'My counsel shall stand, and I will accomplish all my purpose,'

11 calling a bird of prey from the east, the man of my counsel from a far country. I have spoken, and I will bring it to pass; I have purposed, and I will do it.

12 "Listen to me, you stubborn of heart, you who are far from righteousness:

13 I bring near my righteousness; it is not far off, and my salvation will not delay; I will put salvation in Zion, for Israel my glory."

This chapter is such a powerful proclamation of the uniqueness and sovereignty of our God! He is unlike any other and no other person, entity, or deity can compare to Him! (5,8). This is precisely why Isaiah calls the people to listen (3,12), remember (8,9), and stand firm (8). No one else is deserving of our attention more than the one, true God. God, through Isaiah, is calling them to open their ears, take the words to heart, and stand firm ("be a champion") in them.

The puny, competing voices called out in the text are those of Bel and Nebo. These two were chief gods in the collective deities of Babylonia. Their images would be carried at the forefront of parades in Babylon.[15] Babylon was where the Israelites were headed for exile,

---

[15] https://www.studylight.org/commentaries/dcc/isaiah-46.html, accessed April 26, 2020.

so Isaiah is giving a forewarning. When they encountered these other gods and were tempted to bow, they should remember that there is only one true God. Bel and Nebo do not stand a chance against their God.

God makes it clear that the other gods do not even compare. He shows this by actually comparing Himself with the other. I find it helpful to visually see the contrasts. Check out how God points out His unique sovereignty and the false gods' frailty:

God	Bel/Nebo
Glorifies Himself (13)	Bows Down / Stoops (1,2)
Saves (4) / Brings Salvation (13)	Cannot Save (2,7)
Knows from Birth (3) / Is Creator (3,4) / Made (4)	Is Created (6)
Carries from Womb to Old Age (3,4) / Carries (4) / Bears (4)	Is Carried (7)
Accomplishes His Purposes (10,11) / Brings Righteousness (13)	Stands in Place (7) Cannot Move (7)
Calls (11) / Declares End from Beginning (10) / Counsel Stands (10,11)	Cannot Answer (7)

These gods had to be crafted by human hands; yet our God is the One who created humans. These gods had to be carried by human hands; yet our God is the one who carries us from the womb to old age. These gods cannot save; yet our God is the Savior. These gods cannot speak; yet our God not only speaks but declares the end from the beginning with words that never fail. These gods cower before the might and authority of the Almighty Who will glorify Himself through all things.

I hope you understand that we are not simply talking about Bel and Nebo here. This truth cast upon the Israelites through the prophet Isaiah is just as relevant to us today. We may not be dealing with statues of Bel and Nebo, but we are dealing with our own idols.

Question: Do you carry your gods or does your God carry you?

How do we know if we are bearing the burden of idols in our lives? This can be a tricky question to answer as it is often subjective, and we have a tendency to justify our allegiances. However, maybe some exploratory questions would have us better evaluate our lives. I encourage you to go through these questions slowly not haphazardly. Examine them prayerfully, asking God to open your eyes to any of these potential idols in your life.

- Is there anything that you are unwilling to give up?
- Is there anything that is against God's will for your life that you are hanging on to?
  For example...
  > *Pride*
  > *Lust*
  > *Greed*
  > *Self-reliance*
- Is there anything you value over your relationship with the Lord?
  For example...
  > *Relationships*
  > *Wealth*
  > *Health*
  > *Popularity or Reputation*
  > *Material Possessions*
- *What do you need in your life to worship the unseen God?*
  For example...
  > *Rituals*
  > *Icons*
  > *Religious Symbols*
  > *Works-based Religion*

Now, truthfully, idolatry is something that we all struggle with as human beings. We are constantly in a battle against valuing those things that are temporary versus the things which are unseen. The eternal perspective demands that we focus our allegiance on the one, true, invisible God. That is not easy, but it is *vital*. If these idols were merely statues on the shelf, we could more easily cast them out. But the idols that vie for our affection and attention are much more subtle than that. They creep in and dig their claws into our hearts and before we know it, we are trapped. Therefore, we must be diligent, consistently working out our salvation in fear and trembling (Philippians 2:11-13). We must stay alert because the deceptive enemy is trying his best to destroy us, often from the inside out (1 Peter 5:6-9).

Be assured of this: there is nothing in this world that can compare or compete with our awesome Lord. Everything that tries to will ultimately fall miserably short. So, there is no sense in wasting time with the "wannabes." Put all your trust, devotion, and affection into the eternal God and everything else will fall into place (John 6:33).

SECTION 5:

"For the things that are seen are transient but the things that are unseen are eternal."

CHAPTER 21

MASTERING THE ESCAPE ROOM

T HE CLOCK STARTS AT 60 MINUTES AND THE countdown begins. You and a few teammates are locked in a small mysterious room full of artifacts, locked chests, and cryptic puzzles. Your step-by-step challenge is to figure out the mystery that unlocks the door and leads to freedom. This experience weaves together a crazy concoction that is equal parts adrenaline-laced excitement and mind-boggling frustration. Those who give up easily or are prone to quickly throwing in the towel don't stand a chance. However, through the power of teamwork, perseverance, and an open mind, the challenge can be overcome. Every solved puzzle leads to a new challenge.

One of the things I like about escape rooms is the way they mimic this crazy adventure called life. Life is a challenge. No honest person would deny that assertion. There are certainly victories, joys, and times when everything seems to fall into place, but those are often countered with failures, grief, and times when nothing seems to go right. It is a journey mixed with highs and lows, confidence and skepticism, faith and doubt. We pour out tears, sometimes in gratitude and other times because of sorrow.

I love that the Bible does not post the perfect social media picture of life. You know when you delete the 5 pictures that are not as flattering as the one you chose to post. In social media, we only let the public see the "me" we choose for them to see. Usually, it is the one without the flaws or hardships.

That is not how the Bible does it. It is real about the struggles and difficulties we face. Yet, in the midst of that reality check, it never ceases to promote hope. The same Jesus who said, "I have come that they may have life and have it more abundantly" (John 10:10), also stated, "I have said these things to you, that in me you may have peace. In the world you will have tribulation. But take heart; I have overcome the world" (John 16:33). We love to claim the promises of God, right? Well, check out His promise right there in that verse you just read: "In the world you will have tribulation." That is one we would like to skip over. We often spend our time yearning for better times. *Calm the storms and eliminate the hardships, Lord.* Yet trials, tribulations, and trouble in this world is exactly what the Word promises.

So, what is this abundant life that Jesus promises? Is it really about physical blessings? Is it having all the money I want, so I never have to budget again? Is it never having to endure waiting in an emergency department or having to hear the word "cancer?" Is it the absence of relational tension and discontent? Is it achieving all of my dreams and ambitions?

Nice thought, but is that reality? Is that what Jesus promised? You know, this is the same Jesus who often lacked a decent place to sleep and had "no place to lay His head" (Matthew 8:20). The biblical Jesus was consistently ridiculed and mocked. This Jesus was hated, beaten, and crucified.

Or could it be that even in the midst of all the junk that Jesus endured, He still was experiencing abundance in life? Could it be that the abundant life is more about what is happening *within* us than what is happening on the *outside*? How else while suffocating and bleeding on the cross could Jesus have looked down on his persecutors and said, "Father, forgive them, for they know not what they do" (Luke 23:34).

It is a supernatural occurrence when God brings abundant life even in the midst of a world that is falling apart.

Let's look at two examples of abundant life in spite of difficult circumstances, one from the Old Testament and one from the New.

Joseph had it made. Despite being the 11th son out of 12, which would have made him low on the totem pole of family hierarchy, he had the blessing of being Papa Jacob's favorite. He got the most attention, the "favorite kid" status, and the one-of-a-kind coat. He even had a special gift for interpreting dreams. He was special for sure.

He also got the curse of being the focus of his brothers' hatred, built upon the foundational stones of envy and jealousy.

Joseph's life of ease took a hard turn and became one escape room after another. Genesis 39:2 clearly states that "The LORD was with Joseph." But given his life circumstances, one might wonder.

He was thrown into a pit and then sold into slavery to foreigners by his brothers. The traders took him to Egypt where he was sold as a slave to the captain of Pharaoh's guard. Foreign land. Slave. This would be a good time to embrace some pity, to start questioning God, to sink to the bottom of the chasm. What did Joseph do? He became the best servant he could be and in so doing caught the eye of his master. Potiphar ended up putting Joseph in charge of his entire household leaving him virtually carefree.

But Potiphar was not the only one that Joseph made an impression on. Potiphar's wife liked what she saw as well—in a different way. She made a move on Joseph, but he refused out of loyalty to his master and allegiance to his ultimate Master. He made the right choice and where did that get him? Thrown in jail on a false accusation. *"Can I complain now? What good is doing the right thing when it gets you the wrong result?"* Nope, not Joseph. What did he do? He became the best prisoner he could be. He was so responsible that he caught the eye of the head jailer and he put Joseph in charge of all the prisoners! And the jailer had no worries or cares about the jail anymore.

Notice the pattern?

Joseph encounters two fellas in prison who are upset about their dreams. Joseph makes an incredible statement when these guys approach him for help with their dreams. "They said to him, 'We have had dreams, and there is no one to interpret them.' And Joseph said to them, 'Do not interpretations belong to God? Please tell them to me'" (Genesis 40:8). I love this subtle proclamation. Basically, Joseph says, "Only God can interpret dreams and since I am the only one in here who knows the one, true God, go ahead and let me hear them."

The story is not about Joseph; it is about the God of Joseph. So too, your story is not about you! It is about God. Never forget that life principle! Your momentary frustrations in life are all being worked toward a future that glorifies the Creator. We must learn to take our eyes off our prison walls and realize that there are no walls strong enough to contain the glory of God in our lives.

Back to the story. Joseph's dream interpretations came true: the baker died and the cupbearer was restored to his job with Pharaoh. He immediately forgot about Joseph who ended up sitting in prison for another 2 years.

Note what the Word says about Joseph as He was in prison:

> "But the LORD was with Joseph and showed him steadfast love and gave him favor in the sight of the keeper of the prison."
>
> –Gen. 39:21

> "Because the LORD was with him. And whatever he did, the LORD made it succeed."
>
> –Gen. 39:23

Most of us would question how God is making Joseph successful. Wouldn't success mean that things are going his way? But he is sitting in prison for years under false accusations. Most of us wonder where in the world God is when we are in the middle of our difficult circumstances. The truth is that He is right there with us, working in us, working through us, sculpting an incredible story that screams how awesome He is.

In just the right timing, God worked through the cupbearer and the pagan Pharaoh to bring Joseph out of prison and into second in command in Egypt. Why? Was this meant as a compensatory blessing for all that Joseph had to endure? Nope. This was about putting Joseph in just the right place at the right time with the right amount of influence to preserve Israel, and to ultimately bring forth the Savior who would deliver all who believe.

Joseph's life, directed by God, was ultimately about bringing forth the Messiah.

In a complementary way, Paul's life, directed by God, was ultimately about spreading the good news that the Messiah had come!

Paul spent much of his life being the religious authority—judge, jury, and executioner—and made it his mission to wipe out the fledgling movement of those who professed this crucified and risen Savior. Then one day, this risen Savior stopped Paul in his tracks and completely changed the trajectory of his life. He went from being the hunter to the hunted, the persecutor to the persecuted, the self-righteous judge to the humble proclaimer of grace. His life got harder in the temporary, but his confidence in eternal glory outweighed it all. That is why Paul could embrace all of the tribulations he faced and "boast" about his weaknesses he outlined in 2 Corinthians 11:16-30. In Philippians 4:11-13, he states:

> "Not that I am speaking of being in need, for I have
> learned in whatever situation I am to be content.
> I know how to be brought low, and I know how
> to abound. In any and every circumstance, I have

learned the secret of facing plenty and hunger, abundance and need. I can do all things through him who strengthens me."

That last verse has been used to assure people that God will help them accomplish anything they set their minds to. It has been put on billboards, tattooed on chests, and even given as battle cries at sporting events. The verse's context, however, has little to do with our own ambitions and more about God giving us strength to be content no matter what circumstances we face. That is such an encouraging promise and Paul lived in it.

Back to the escape room, here is another aspect that cannot be overlooked. There is someone watching you while you are trying to figure the room out. This is someone who knows all of the secrets of the room, every puzzle and every solution. You can even ask him/her for hints. They are willing to guide without providing all of the answers at once.

This journey of life is an escape room, full of twists and turns, difficulties, and struggles. But there is also a Lord who is in control. He is always there. He knows every puzzle and every solution. He won't give you all of the answers at once, for that would diminish the journey and also give less opportunity for His power to be displayed.

God's glory was what Joseph's life was all about. It is what Paul's life was all about. And that is what your life is all about. Until we embrace the truth of our existence, we will never see past the prison walls of circumstance. Our difficulties are merely the platforms for God to show off His glory.

CHAPTER 22

PARKING DECK THEOLOGY

WHAT BETTER PLACE TO GET A PICTURE OF OUR journey through life than a parking deck? Sound a bit crazy? Let me explain.

On a recent hospital visit, I proceeded into a parking deck driving my old, 1991, red Buick. You undoubtedly have experienced these massive concrete structures designed to cram as many cars as possible into confined spaces and stress out the more claustrophobic among us. I knew as I pulled in that day that I was in for a real treat...well, not really. As soon as I saw this other similarly aged Buick in front of me, I figured this guy was not as comfortable as I was in the Buick beast in tight parking deck lanes. This guy was really taking his time. I think he had accepted the challenge to see exactly how slow he could go and still keep the car rolling without stopping. It was painful and tested that special fruit of the Spirit that often hides out in the back of my heart's pantry: patience.

On my very next trip to the hospital about a week later, I had an encounter that was the same...only different. That time I was not plagued by a sluggish old Buick driver. No, that time it was "Mr. Dragway" in his hooped-up Mustang. Unbelievable! I came around the corner heading up and this guy was flying on his way down. He cut the corner right in front of me. I guess he wanted to get out of the deck a good 0.0001 seconds sooner. I slammed my brakes. He narrowly missed my front bumper. I was stunned. I looked at him with probably not the godliest expression on my face only to see him staring back at me in utter contempt, wielding a hand gesture that seemed to indicate he thought I was number 1! *My deepest apologies for staying in my own lane sir while you try to take up both of ours.*

What is wrong with people? What is wrong with us? What is wrong with me? You see, in life we struggle in similar ways to that parking deck.

Sometimes, we are just gradually meandering from one mundane habitual task to the other. We are too nervous to act out of the routine. We are too hesitant to make a decision. We avoid risks at all points. Sometimes we take on a posture where uncertainty of the outcome creates inertia.

But what about when God is calling us to do something, and we are too timid to step up and embrace the risk. We examine the pros and cons and are just filled with too much doubt. We wait and wait. We cannot clearly state what we are waiting for, and we are paralyzed.

What would have happened if Abraham had stayed put when God told him to start walking, destination to be determined? *(Genesis 12)*. What would have been the results if Moses left the burning bush and headed to the comfort zone of home instead of God's call to the hostile foreign land? *(Exodus 3-4)*. What opportunity would have been missed if the three young Israelites would have bowed to King Nebuchadnezzar's statue because the cost of standing was too high? *(Daniel 3)*.

What harsh consequences awaited Israel when they decided that God's call to enter the Promised Land was not enough to outweigh the dangers? *(Exodus 13-14)*. What national impact came when Achan decided he simply could not walk away from the spoils of war? *(Joshua 7)*. What lives were affected by Jonah's choice to take a boat in the opposite direction of God's calling? *(Jonah 1)*.

When God tells us to move, we better get our act together and put our engines into gear. You might be thinking: "Ok, I'm willing, but I don't know what He wants me to do or where He wants me to go." Sure you do. Until you have further instructions, do what you know He has called you to do. Try these ever-present instructions on for size. Love God with all that you are. And while you are at it, love your neighbor as yourself *(Matthew 22:37-40)*. Be a witness for Jesus through your testimony and the gospel *(Matthew 18:18-20; Acts 1:8)*. Walk by faith, not by sight *(2 Corinthians 5:7)*. Be humble, just like Jesus *(Philippians 2:1-11; 1 Peter 5:5-7)*. Seek to serve others, just like Jesus *(John 13)*. And the list goes on.

Often, we spend too much time looking for that special word from the Lord, all the while neglecting the clear Word He has given us. Don't hesitate on what He has said. Move!

On the other hand, however, sometimes it is not the lack of speed in our lives, it is the unwise overabundance of acceleration that gets us in trouble. This happens when we jump first and ask questions later. Our mouths outrun the filters on our brains. We can act on impulse with a goal to make sure no moment is wasted. We can get ahead of God's calling and timing, severely handicapping the purpose of our lives.

What miracle would have been missed if Jesus had not tarried 2 extra days before heading to see Lazarus at the tomb? *(John 11)*. What would have happened to the spread of the gospel if the disciples had not waited in the upper room for the Holy Spirit to fall on them and had rushed out into the mission with their own strength? *(Acts 2)*. What would have occurred if Paul had resisted the urge of the Spirit and had stayed on his planned route because he had his own travel itinerary? *(Acts 16)*.

What millennia-old conflict resulted from Abram and Sarai coming up with an alternative plan when waiting for the promised child seemed too difficult? *(Genesis 16)*. What tragic predicament could have been avoided if Jephthah had just been confident in the

Lord's presence rather than make such a rash vow? *(Judges 11)*. What difficulties could David had avoided if he had been leading his army into battle rather than staying home and acting on his lust from his rooftop? *(2 Samuel 11,12)*.

When God tells us to wait, we need to slow our roll. Patience, after all, is not just a virtue; it is one evidence of the Holy Spirit at work in the believer *(Galatians 5:22)*. We need to be careful to obey the Spirit's blinking "No Crossing" sign before we jaywalk into a mess of life's traffic.

When does God tell us to pump the breaks? Be slow to speak and to anger *(James 1:19-20)*. Be steadfast or persevere in difficult times *(Romans 5:2-3; Colossians 1:23; James 1:12)*. Never lose hope in the waiting *(2 Peter 3:11-13)*.

As with most things in life, balance between waiting and running is the key.

> *But they who wait for the LORD shall renew their*
> *strength; they shall mount up with wings like eagles; they*
> *shall run and not be weary; they shall walk and not faint.*
> *—Isaiah 40:31*

"Isaiah's prophecies came in between the Assyrian conquering and exiling the northern kingdom of Israel and the eventual conquering and exiling of the southern kingdom of Judah by Babylon. He prophesies against the ungodliness of the kingdoms that had been created by God for God's glory. God's judgement would come upon his children who had prostituted themselves with neighboring pagan nations and traditions."[16]

But God would not destroy them; rather, He would bring them back. The Israelites would grow weary and lose hope in the midst of

---

[16] W. E. Vine, "Vine's Expository Commentary on Isaiah" (Nashville: Thomas Nelson Publishers, 1997), 3-4.

exile. They would grow faint. However, in the midst of their grief in enduring the discipline of the Lord at the hands of a pagan nation, God would never stop working. God told them, through Isaiah, that He was still the One on the throne. He was going to bring them back and bring restoration. They needed to wait on Him and, in so doing, He would revitalize their strength, enabling them to soar, run, and walk.

Waiting is not intended to be a complacent and lazy demeanor. It is not meant to create inaction or paralyze. It is an eager and hopeful waiting. It is the posture of a basketball player facing off against his opponent for a jump ball. He is crouched and ready to spring up once the ball has been launched. Waiting is like the sprinter on the blocks awaiting the gun. Waiting is like the action of the farmer who is patiently anticipating the coming crop, but watering and tending to the ground in the meantime (James 5:7).

Soaring, running, and walking in Isaiah's prophecy are not intended to be with hasty actions, absent of direction and discernment. Eagles don't soar without their God-given wings. We are not meant to run on weary and exhausted legs. When God empowers us to walk again, fainting will be a distant memory. No athlete goes immediately into the competition and succeeds. Months, and even years, of practice are involved to train the body for battle. No soldier goes into battle untrained. If he does, he will be picked off quickly.

Therefore, we wait on the Lord. We wait with a hope and a faith that are secure in Him and His promises. We use the time in waiting to grow deeper into Him. We don't waste our time while waiting. We stay active, doing the things He has called us to do. When a new God-given assignment arises then we will cast aside fear and doubt and run with force into the fray. We can do this because through faithfulness and perseverance in the waiting, God has equipped us with the strength, gifts, wisdom, and discernment necessary to accomplish the mission.

There you have it. The parking deck of life. Don't let the size of life's structure either intimidate you or squeeze you in. Because God is greater, we can move through life without fear. But don't let confidence in yourself or your own abilities make you reckless. Taking those turns too fast on your own could prove disastrous. Wait for Him to do His work *in* you so that He can do His work *through* you.

CHAPTER 23

STUCK IN THE IN-BETWEEN

M Y NAME IS BILL, AND I WAS A CARD-CARRYING member of Daters Anonymous. Now, don't get it wrong: I was not a Dating Addict; rather, it was the opposite. Let me explain.

Growing up, my teen years were exciting and fun. I was fairly popular, which translates to: I had a lot of friends from all walks of life and no known enemies. I made people laugh, due to my willingness to be silly in public and give quick funny comebacks. (Actually, that part is still true!) I was rarely lonely and had a pretty full social life. What I did not have was a lot of girlfriends. Don't misunderstand, I had a lot of friends who were girls, but not many "girlfriends." I had my own insecurities about why that was but looking back I think the biggest reason was my near refusal to ask girls out and often the mere thought of it bringing on paralysis! The stakes were seemingly too high. The potential pain of rejection was not worth the risk of asking. The few times I actually revealed some interest in a girl I got one of 2 outcomes: Either the interest was returned only for me to shortly thereafter realize that I had been more interested in the chase than the actual person, or the revelation of my interest got me mule-kicked over the cliff into Rejection Canyon, which felt much deeper and intimidating than the Grand Canyon itself. I remember being so jealous of those guys who were so forward with girls. They seemed so confident that they simply didn't care what the response was.

Eventually, we realize that each of our journeys is unique. Each journey is specifically overseen by the Lord. We have different paths, and the "Super-Dater" was not mine. Even up to the Spring semester of my senior year in college, I was not sure if I would ever find that great romantic love. However, God, in His perfect timing, finally led me to my bride, the love of my life, and it was worth the wait. Seeing her beauty come through those church doors in her wedding bliss will be forever etched in my mind. If my memory serves me right, she even had a halo that day. It was a defining moment that laid any lingering fears I had of never making it out of the friend zone!

The journey from conception to final breath can be a crazy and confusing path. It often can feel like the frustrating maze of the "in-be-tween." All we can see is the wall or obstacle immediately in front of us. In our limited perspective, we can't see the bigger picture.

Picture for a moment walking casually into unfamiliar woods looking for a lake you heard had some great fishing. It is located deep in the woods, but you have a map. Yet, the further you advance, glancing from the map to the woods in front of you just brings greater disori-entation. With each leaf-crunching step, you simply see one tree after another. You have been told this lake is incredible, but you are starting to doubt whether it even exists at all.

Now imagine that you set down your backpack. After taking a swig of water, you unzip the main pocket and pull out your mini drone, start it up, link it to your phone and send it up through the tops of the trees. As the drone breaks through the canopy, all of a sudden you are intro-duced to a completely new perspective. As you scan above the trees, you realize that you are only about 100 yards from the lake. The destination is perfectly visible—with the right perspective.

One biblical witness of this perspective can be found in Jeremiah 29:11. Here we have a verse that is often quoted, though I must say it is generally used out of context. It says, "For I know the plans I have for you, declares the LORD, plans for welfare and not for evil, to give you a future and a hope." Many have plastered this on their walls and notebooks and shirts as a specific promise to them from the Lord. It is not. Whenever we divorce a single verse from its context, we run the risk of misinterpretation. The truth is that God was delivering a message through Jeremiah that was specific to the people of Israel. *(Hang with me now, there is a relevant application for us.)*

If we read Jeremiah 29 as a whole, we get the context. God had used Babylon to conquer the southern kingdom of Israel (Judah) and carry them away into captivity. They had been warned by the Lord and yet they continued to prostitute themselves with pagan people and gods. So, God disciplined them for His glory and their own good. Exile became a part of their journey.

They found themselves exiled in Babylonia: a broken and displaced people. As Jeremiah prophesied to these exiles, we see a challenge, a promise, and a prophecy.

He challenged them to make Babylon better by their presence. Imagine the audacity. Babylon had persecuted, plundered, and abducted them. They were to respond by being the nice guys? They were to build houses and plant gardens, marry and multiply. They were to pray for the city and its welfare. In addition, they were to stop listening to the false prophets who were spewing prophecies that had no basis in God's truth. (vv. 4-9)

Then comes the promise. In 70 years, the Lord was going to do something spectacular. He was going to turn the tide and bring the exiles home, back to Jerusalem. What they were experiencing in their immediate circumstances was not the full story or the final chapter. Even when it seemed like God was as far off as another galaxy, He was still at work in their midst.

This is where that key verse 11 comes in: *"For I know the plans I have for you, declares the Lord, plans for welfare and not for evil, to give you a future and a hope.*" God was basically telling the exiles several truths. He knew His plans and it was not what the lie-talkers are spewing. Amid their exile and difficulty, His plans were for their welfare, for their future, for their hope. Ultimately, this is about the preservation of the remnant of Israel to eventually bring forth the Messiah. Despite what they heard, God was still on the throne, in charge, and His purposes would come to fruition.

This promise was coupled with the prophecy. They would call on Him and He would hear. They would seek Him and would find Him. And in that process, He would restore everything back to them that they had lost. Such grace!

It would not be wise to make this verse about us when it was clearly a *specific* promise to a *specific* people in the midst of a *specific* situation. However, there are some themes in this verse we see throughout the Bible.

God knows where we are and where He is taking us. If God were a batter, He could never be fooled by the pitch. Every changeup or curveball is a home run waiting to happen. Unlike us, He is not surprised by what happens to us. He is not perplexed by the circumstances surrounding us. He is not confused by the blindside hits we take.

For believers in Jesus, He promised us an eternal future and a hope that will be devoid of evil (Colossians 3:1-11; Revelation 21-22). He promised that our troubles and tribulations will not be wasted but are actually working in us and through us to produce a glory that outweighs everything (2 Corinthians 4:17). He promised us a Kingdom that is eternal and that we can know we will be there with Him forever (John 14:3-4; 1 John 5:11-13). He promised us a glorified body, sin-free, immortal, and imperishable. (1 Corinthians 15:42-44)

You might be reading these truths and think, "That is all well and good. When heaven gets here, I will be glad. But what about now?! How do I get through this moment?"

How do we navigate the in-between? Where is the job I need? Where is the soul mate I yearn for? Where is the repentance of a friend who betrayed me? Where is the financial break-through I am desperate for? Where is the peace I crave? Where is the direction I am seeking?

Sometimes the in-between can stretch you to the absolute breaking point.

Let me encourage you through whatever "in-between" you are experiencing by getting a little personal. You see, my daughter, Alaina, at the time of this writing, is in one of those in-between stages. She is 21 and halfway through here senior year in college. As many of her friends are getting engaged and married and planning careers, she feels stuck and uncertain. She longs for that person to share her life with, but there are no current prospects. She wants clear direction on an occupation, but she has no clarity on what that looks like. As much as she is excited for the happiness and plans of her friends, she begins to wonder if something is wrong with her for not having all of her future life figured out. *Ugh.* The in-between is not for cowards.

You may not be in Alaina's specific situation, but you no doubt have had or are currently having your own in-between seasons. So, for that reason, I offer you what I offer my daughter, in hopes that it touches a part of your heart, as well. And yes, this book will be around long after this season passes for her, but that is exactly why I include it. This is a faith milestone marker to look back and see clearly how God knew what He was doing even in the darker times.

Dear Alaina,

Your Mom and I are so proud of the young woman you have become. You have successfully navigated through so many of life's journeys and struggles with the Lord on the throne. Your risk-taking, adventurous, and mission-mindedness thrills my heart. I know that you are in the midst of a difficult in-between season. You work so hard on your plans and making sure that everything is in order. Your "lists" are legendary! Because of this, I know this time is especially frustrating for you.

Life is seemingly moving on for others and your path lacks clarity. Though graduation is an anticipated achievement, you are viewing it with a little anxiety due to the uncertainty of your future. This reality weighs heavy on your Mom and me, as well. We want you to be happy, excited, and confident. When you are hurting, frustrated or struggling, we bear the weight of those emotions with you.

But take heart! The in-between is not meant to be just a season to endure and get to the other side. It is a time of faith-building and preparation. It is the cocoon in the process of your maturing. It can be painful, but the hurt is not wasted. It can be frustrating, but the irritations are not wasted. It is all part of the journey...a journey that will reap great rewards spiritually, emotionally, physically, mentally, and socially.

In the meantime: Cast your net wide and see what unexpected opportunities come your way. Dig deep into the Word and prayer and prioritize your relationship with your Savior. Serve God well by serving others well. Pick your head up and maintain a focus on the things that last forever.

And soon, when you get to the other side—when career aspirations are solidified, when you have found that special someone, when life seems to finally be clicking—don't forget the in-between.

For without the in-between, the sweetness of the other side would be without any noticeable flavor.

I love you, Dad ("Doodie")

Chapter 24

All In

PREPARE YOURSELF FOR WHAT IS TO COME. SOME of you reading this will embrace what you are about to read. Others will be offended, dismayed, and maybe even put this book down for good. *(Maybe that is why I saved it until the end!)* I have literally had people leave my church over what I am getting ready to share with you. But it is worth the risk.

Several years ago, I came under conviction that nearly all of my time was spent with church folk. This is not necessarily a bad thing. After all, as a pastor, I am called to shepherd a body of believers. Being a shepherd of a church means, among a myriad of responsibilities, being a servant leader pointing to the Great Shepherd, teaching believers, comforting the hurting, encouraging the distraught, and walking in love with them through the highs and lows of life. However, when I would preach passionately on evangelism, it would always leave me a little uneasy that my schedule was so consumed with the needs of church people that I was rarely out in the world engaging people who did not know Jesus.

So, I began to actively pray and seek out a place where I could engage people on their turf. The following account displays how God answered that prayer.

I was looking at a member's Facebook page one day and saw one of her friends who was in a wheelchair. I felt a strong tugging at my heart. Maybe this was the Lord was leading me to meet this girl. I spoke to my member and she said, "Oh, that is my atheist friend." Perfect. I asked her to discreetly see if I could meet her. Her discreet way of handling it was to call her friend and say, "My pastor wants to meet you." Really?! Well, her friend skeptically said that her dad was in the hospital having surgery the next day and I could come by if I didn't "preach" at them.

So, I showed up the next day in the waiting room and chatted with her and her mom for 2 hours. Through that, a friendship was birthed that led to many intriguing and deep conversations over the years. We never got into heated arguments, but we never held back either. I wish I could say that she came around to faith in Christ, but I cannot. What I can say is that the gospel of Jesus was proclaimed to her in word, deed, and lifestyle. I can also say that I shattered her stereotype of Christians being hypocritical, arrogant, ignorant, fairy-tale followers.

But something else happened through that encounter. She worked at a bar that hosted free poker tournaments every week. I decided to carry the light into the darkness of that environment. I was honest with my congregation about what I was doing. The last thing I needed was someone to start a rumor about seeing the preacher headed into the bar. I made my congregation repeat after me: "When Pastor Bill goes to play poker in the bar, he does not drink [alcohol] or gamble." For many that brought a chuckle. For others, it brought confrontation and condemnation. I literally had people tell me that I was destroying my witness by engaging in that environment. They stated that if I wanted to evangelize, then door to door was the primary acceptable method.

I asked one of my critics if he thought Jesus would be in a place like that. "Heaven's no!" was the response I got. Really? To the contrary, one of the big criticisms of Jesus was that He hung out too much with sinners.

*"Now the tax collectors and sinners were all drawing heart
to hear him. And the Pharisees and the scribes grumbled,
saying 'This man receives sinners and eats with them.'"
–Luke 15:1-2*

*"And as he reclined at the table in his house, many tax
collectors and sinners were reclining with Jesus and his
disciples, for there were many who followed him. And the
scribes of the Pharisees, when they saw that he was eating
with sinners and tax collectors, said to his disciples, 'Why
does he eat with tax collectors and sinners?' And when
Jesus heard it, he said to them, 'Those who are well have
no need of a physician, but those who are sick. I came
not to call the righteous, but sinners.'" –Mark 2:15-17*

In reading Jesus' words, we must remember that none are righteous on their own accord (Romans 3:9-12,23). He was not saying that the religious leaders were righteous and outside the need of His grace. He was inferring that as long as they considered themselves to be self-sufficiently holy, then they would never understand their need for Him. The sick need a doctor. The sinner needs a Savior. Seeking and saving is why Jesus came (Luke 19:10).

So, whether my brothers and sisters could understand or not, I went into the fray. I didn't go recklessly or unwisely. I didn't go into a place where I would be flooded with temptation. This would not be a good mission for someone who struggled with alcoholism. I went with my guard up, my armor on, and my church family praying for me.

And I went somewhat covertly, at first. I didn't barge into the bar saying, "Hide the beer, the pastor's here!" On the contrary, I was stepping into their territory. I engaged in very casual conversation with other players. No one asked what I did for a living and I didn't offer that information up. I was intentional about this. The people I meet in venues like this often have preconceived stereotypes of Christians and especially Pastor/Preachers; therefore, my goal was to build relationships first before the "big reveal." Building relationships first helps to minimize the obstacles to deeper relationships once people know what I do.

The other thing I had to do was to actually gain some "poker cred." That means I needed to win some of these free tournaments. When you start to win some of the tournaments, you begin to tear down walls. In other words, more people actually want to talk with you. Honestly, if you stink at poker, you are not going to get too far with this group. After a while, inevitably, it came out that I am a pastor. This would usually start when I would ask someone how I could pray for them. The initial reactions I get when that subject is broached can often be quite comical to me. Shortly after that point, as word spread, I become somewhat of an unofficial chaplain of the bar.

I could write an entire book on the encounters I have had over the years playing poker in bars. God really showed up in crazy ways.

Like Chuck:

Me: So, Chuck, is there anything I can pray about for you?

Chuck: (Shifts his head up toward me and looks at me like an alien had just taken over my body.) What?! (His whole demeanor changed. He was truly blindsided with this question.)

Me: Well, I pray, and I was just wondering if there was anything I could pray about for you.

C: Well, I reckon not!

M: Ok. That's cool.

C: What are you, some kind of big-time Christian?

M: Uh...I'm A Christian.

C: I'll be honest with you, man, I'm not very religious. I really have a problem with organized religion. I grew up in a poor neighborhood and all I know of Christians was that they were all about money. The pastors made promises but never delivered and they always seemed to take from the poor for their own benefit. So, I've never had a good taste in my mouth for Christians.

M: That kind of thing really saddens me and makes me angry too, bro. There is no doubt that Christians and pastors can get it wrong, flipping it all around for their own benefit rather than the benefit of others. That is not the way it is supposed to be. I aim to break your stereotype that those folks have given you about pastors.

C: Oh, really?? (Looking skeptically at me.)

M: Yep. You see, I'm a pastor. Jesus said that He did not come to be served but to serve and give his life as a ransom for many. That is what I'm striving to do.

Thus began a relationship where Charlie started coming to me often for prayer for his family.

Like Krystal:

One day she started staring daggers at me from across the table. I could feel it and it was awkward. I finally made eye contact with her and kind of smirked as I nodded my head. She said, "I don't feel right cussing around you." She did not mean that as a compliment. I said, "Don't change your

167

language for me. I'm not offended." You see, from an eternal perspective, Karla's need for Jesus was much more important than her need for a washed-out mouth.

After that game, she came over to me and blessed me out. She was livid and delivered some pretty harsh blows about Christians and pastors. I patiently took every shot she pounded me with. When her rant had run its course, I asked her, "I am sorry you feel the way you feel. What happened that made you so hostile toward pastors?" She started crying and said that her father had been a pastor but left the ministry when he left his family for another woman. Things began to make sense.

That began a relationship that led to me counseling her lesbian daughter, not in the bar but in my church office!

Like Hammer:

This young man had a normal name but preferred to go by Hammer to make sure folks knew how tough he was. He was loud and aggressive.

One day, I pulled him aside and said, "Hey Hammer, how can I pray for you." He bowed up his chest and laughed deeply.

"Man, I don't need prayer."

I said, "Well, I'm going to pray for you anyway, I was just going to give you an opportunity to tell me something specific I can lift up."

In that moment, something miraculous happened. The bravado faded for a brief moment. The warrior became a child. In a small voice, just above a whisper, with a look of hurt in his eyes, he said, "Pray that I can get my life together." Seemingly, before a tear could flow, the mask went back up as quickly as it had come down. He walked away loudly proclaiming how cool and tough he was. But for that moment, God forced the veil to be lowered.

Like Tom:

Tom is deaf. We started text messaging at the table on breaks. He made it clear that he was an atheist. I didn't let up, I kept praying for him, and kept talking to him. Years later, he messaged that he had put his faith in Christ and sent me pictures of him being baptized.

Like Brody:

Brody, sitting next to me at the poker table, asked me to marry he and his fiancé even though he was adamant that he was not into organized religion. He did not think pre-marital counseling was necessary because they lived together. I told him, "I have three responses to that. 1) Couples who cohabitate prior to marriage have a higher divorce rate than those who do not; 2) Pre-marital counseling reveals as much or more about yourself as it does about the other person; 3) If you want me to do the wedding, it is required; non-negotiable." What I didn't reveal at that point, was that it was going to provide me 6 sessions of gospel-impacting time with him.

That same Brody eventually put his faith in Jesus and is now growing in the Lord, serving with a youth group at a church.

I could go on and on. There have been so many encounters in this environment. I've been cussed at and appreciated. I've had folks ask me for prayer and I have had others tell me to keep my religion to myself. I have encouraged other Christians and debated with atheists. I have been sought out and I have been ignored and avoided. I've seen some come to faith and many reject it.

But at the end of the day, it is my job to simply be a witness and a herald to the greatest news in all of eternity: the gospel. Ultimately, I'm just trying to be like Jesus. There is a way to get into these environments and shine the brightest light where the darkness thrives. There is a way to be amongst sinners while not letting the sin stains of the world get on us.

It is why we remain on earth in this moment.

Worship will be in heaven.
Fellowship with believers will be in heaven.
Proclamation of the Word of God will be in heaven.
Creative expression will be heaven.
Serving the body will be in heaven.

However, even though the gospel is eternal, sharing the gospel to the lost is a temporary earthly endeavor. We only do it here. So, make the most of the time here in preparation for the eternity to come.

Find what you love to do and make it a mission.

It's time to lay your cards on the table and go all in.

CHAPTER 25

WHEN LIFE MAKES NO SENSE

EVERYTHING WAS PERFECT. THE YEAR WAS 1970. Beth and Ralph had sealed their love with marriage vows and now in their early 20's, their dreams were coming true as they found out she was pregnant. Ralph's heart had been damaged by an early childhood disease and had caused him problems ever since. They knew he was not guaranteed a long life, but their love was rich, and they eagerly awaited the day they could together hold their coming child.

It was not to be. Ralph died of heart disease. Beth, just three months pregnant, was left by herself with grief as her closest companion. Her doctor advised that abortion was an option, after all, raising a child on her own was a lot more than she bargained for. A heart was broken. A dream was shattered. Everything had changed. How could she face this trial?

What do we do when trials come out of nowhere and steamroll us like a freight train?

At the tender age of 26, I conducted my first funeral. It was for a parent of a teenager I had pastored. He had given his life to Jesus and been miraculously transformed and rescued from drug addiction. He was so on fire for the Lord that he made other Christians nervous! He longed to see other addicts, especially the ones he used to hang around with, come to Jesus. He started going back into those dead areas to try to bring life. Sadly, in the process, despite the best of intentions, he succumbed to the lure of his old demons and began using again. One night when he was high, he pulled out his shotgun and started shooting holes in the wall of his home. His wife and kids fled to safety. The cops showed up. He came out into his driveway with his shotgun under his chin and pulled the trigger.

What could I say that would make sense of that tragedy?

The second funeral I had was for a young man in his early 20's. He was engaged to a girl in my church. He was riding his motorcycle and sought to pass a car as it was cresting a hill. He was met with an 18-wheeler head on.

What could I say that would make sense of that tragedy?

Years later, I was awakened at 5am by a phone call from a desperate mom. Just the day before, she had delivered her beautiful baby boy. I had visited them in the hospital. He was having complications because not all of his organs were as developed as they should have been. We thanked God for the gift of life and prayed for God to take care of him and heal him in the NICU. Her words, however, on that morning before the sun had arisen, shook me. She said, "We are keeping him breathing artificially until you get here." I arrived and walked into the NICU to meet them. As tears streamed down our faces, we held that precious boy until he breathed his last breath here on earth.

What could I say that would make sense of that tragedy?

Those are just a few of the many funerals I have overseen. Those are just the funerals...what about all of the other difficulties life throws our way? Parents receive news of a school shooting that has injured their child. A wife is confronted with the desertion of her husband for another woman. The bills have somehow grown to outweigh income. The loss of a job, physical pain, prolonged suffering, excessive grief, and unbearable temptation.

In my pastoring for over 25 years, I sometimes feel like I have seen it all. I've counseled the lesbian atheist. I walked with some of my people through pre-marital counseling to marital bliss to marital dissolution.

I've stood alongside parents going through a custody battle. I've cried with the grieving. I've held the hand of the person struggling to grasp the news they just heard of a terminal illness.

The truth is that when it all turns upside down and nothing makes sense, I don't know what to say. I've found that statements of truth still need to be carefully served on platters of gentleness in these situations. Simple statements like the following tend to fall on deaf ears when the mind is cloudy with the fog of grief, doubt, and despair:

- God has a plan.
- It will all work out.
- It could be worse.
- Hang in there, it will get better.

Believers know that these statements are true, however, when our faith gets severely tested as we go through these difficulties and we don't see Him immediately making the situation right, it is incredibly hard. *If He truly is all-powerful and all-good and all-loving, why doesn't He fix this situation? Where is the justice of God? Has He forgotten about us? Does He even care?* We don't offend Him by asking such questions. He understands.

The questions and feelings are understandable. These are questions we ask about our own plight, but they could have an even farther reach than that. They are expressed every day around the globe.

- Why are Christians being hunted down and slaughtered for their faith in communist and Muslim countries?
- Why are girls being trafficked into the slave and sex trade, not just from the poorest nations, but right here in America?
- Why are there children starving around the world when we spend more on diet products in America annually than it would take to feed everyone in the world?

- Why do murderers get away on technicalities in our legal system?

I could go on and on but suffice it to say: there is a lot of unfairness and injustice going on in our world. It's one thing to be grieved by it theoretically on the global scale. It's grief on a deeper level when it hits in your own home.

Whether it is us or someone we know who is in the middle of these difficulties, our presence and compassion is often better than our words. When we are not in the middle of these heart-breaking times, though, we need to be digging our anchors deep into truth so that we can be prepared to weather the storms when they hit us. It is the answers we know for sure that steady us when we don't have answers to the specific "why."

Here are a few firm foundational truths that we can stand on when life doesn't make sense.

- **God's Glory.** There is no circumstance or situation in which God cannot ultimately bring about His glory. And, frankly, nothing else matters (Psalm 57:5,11; Philippians 2:9-11; 1 Timothy 1:16-17; Revelation 21:23).

- **Eternity.** You and I were made for eternity. Anything we encounter on this earth, good or bad, easy or difficult, joyful or grieving, is temporary. The good is but a shadow of what is to come (Hebrews 11:13-16). The struggles are more than just something we endure, they are allowing us to achieve a glory that far outweighs it all (2 Corinthians 4:17).

- **Sin.** God created the world, Adam, and Eve as perfect, without stain. Man messed it up and introduced sin into the world. It immediately had grave consequences as the 2nd man on earth murdered the 3rd man on earth, his brother. Sin breaking into the world changed everything. And now, we often suffer the natural consequences of our sin. In addition, and sometimes harder to accept, we suffer as victims of the sins of others. Nevertheless, there can be hope in our suffering (Romans 5:3-5).

- **Justice.** Just because God has not acted *yet* to eliminate evil does not mean He has let go. There is coming a day when God will destroy all evil. When He does, everything that is attached to evil will be done away with—cast into Hell forever. That also means that at the point God deals a final blow to evil there will be no eternal hope for anyone who has not placed his or her faith in Christ (Revelation 20:15). God has not yet dealt the final blow to evil because of His love and grace, willing that none should perish. He is giving people more time to come to Him (2 Peter 3:9).

- **Defeated Enemy.** Satan is a powerful enemy. The Bible even calls him the prince of the power of the air (Ephesians 2:2). At the same time, he is living on death row. His end is determined, and he will be the first cast into hell to suffer, mind you, not to rule. In fact, hell was created for Satan's eternal punishment. The unrepentant people that follow him there do so on their own choosing (John 3:16-21). So, though it may appear that he is winning some battles, he is the ultimate loser (Revelation 20:9-10).

- **Our Good.** It is true that God can work everything for the good for believers (Rom. 8:28). Joseph in the book of Genesis was:
  o Beaten up by his brothers.
  o Tossed in a pit.
  o Sold into slavery.
  o Falsely accused of rape and put in jail for years in a foreign nation (Egypt).

Yet God used the sin of others to put Joseph in exactly the position he needed to be in to basically save the entire nation of Israel from famine. God sees the whole picture and He can take the worst of circumstances and use them for our good and His glory (John 16:33).

- **Faith.** It may seem easy to say such things, but harder to put into practice. You may even be thinking, "I don't care about Joseph, I care about my hurt!" I understand, but you and I are helpless in situations like this and casting these cares on Him by faith is our *only* option. Faith is trusting and believing in Him even when things don't make sense to us. Faith is believing that God can and will make things right even when we don't know how or when. Faith is releasing what we are powerless to control anyway (Hebrews 11:1; 1 Peter 5:7).

- **The Body of Christ.** God gave us the church as a community of faith to stand together. We can't necessarily make everything better, but we can give support and encouragement and be a sounding board to one another. We are all in the process of growing and it is hard. We are better together (Hebrews 10:23-25).

Nothing in here is meant to be the final word that makes everything automatically understandable and right. It is just about grounding the foundation of our faith in truth, handling the things we can, and letting go of the things we can't. We trust Him when everything around us seems to be falling apart. And above all, living in light of eternity.

Which brings us back to where we started: Beth. This young woman in her early 20's was 3 months pregnant, and her husband had just died. Her resources were limited, her heart was rent into pieces and she was struggling to figure everything out.

But she was not confused. In the midst of her grief, she knew the Rock upon which she stood:

> She didn't know how she would pay the bills, but she knew the life inside of hers was created by God.

> She didn't have anyone to bring her crackers when the morning sickness hit, but she knew God didn't make mistakes.

> She didn't have another person to share those tender moments of "put your hand here and feel him kick," but she knew her heavenly Father would see her through.

What she could not have known in those days, though, was that the boy growing inside of her would one day be a pastor, a seminary professor, a missionary, and the one who is composing on this computer the very words you are reading.

Thanks Mom, not just for saving my life, but instilling my faith.

Even during the struggles we face where everything seems out of place and nothing makes sense, what *does* make sense is maintaining faith in the eternal God who holds it all together for His glory and our good.

A Cautionary Conclusion

THE DANGER OF AN
ETERNAL PERSPECTIVE

I T MAY SOUND STRANGE, ESPECIALLY COMING FROM me, that having an eternal perspective could have any dangers. After all, I am wholeheartedly committed to this way of viewing life. And that commitment is not just a personal preference. I truly believe that this is a victorious posture and perspective that God calls us to. I see it all over His Word and one day we will see clearly that which is unseen today. It will be glorious! So, what could possibly be a danger with it?

Before I answer that, let me set it up with this relevant funny story.

Mark has many gifts, but there is a particular one that makes a significant impact in my life. He has the unique ability to come up with crazy practical jokes.

When Mark served at a fairly large church, he stretched my ability to pull off a joke every time his church would hire a new staff member. He would let the person get settled into their job for a few months before he would call me to come down for a "mission."

He would give me a primer on the scenario when I got there. I would have about 5-10 minutes to adapt to the role before showtime. He had me playing everything from a praise team applicant to a wall stability specialist to a landscaper looking for a contract to a traveling youth evangelist (complete with cloak and a King James Bible). Each time I would go down there, the other staff members who knew me would crouch in corners and hallways just to listen in on the shenanigans. An entire book could be written about the endeavors, which are still some of the funniest stories to retell in groups years later.

One time, he had me come and meet with their Assimilation Director. My part was to be a "new attender" who was looking for my place to plug into the church. In our encounter, I told her about my gift of prophecy, which meant I would need to be part of the preaching team. I made clear that I was not trying to take over the pulpit. I just would need 1-2 Sundays to preach each month. Can you imagine what was going through her head: *the nerve and absurdness of this newbie's request!* She was calm and cool in answering my hilarious questions and comments.

Then, in the middle of our meeting, I stopped everything and utilized some vital information Mark had given me. My hand went out toward her like I was blessing her while my eyes looked heavenward. I said, "Wait a minute, I'm getting the sense that you have been having some pain." I briefly glanced down at her and her eyes were locked on me. My eyes went back up and I continued. "It seems to be joint related—upper body—have you been having shoulder pain?" I made eye contact. Her eyes were wide open with a curious and surprised expression on her face.

After a few seconds, she said, "Yes, I have."

I replied. "That is what I thought the Lord was telling me."

That was supposed to be it, but her next question threw me a curveball. She asked, "Well, what did the Lord tell you about it?"

The first thing out of my mouth was, "It's gonna be a'ight." I asked her if I could pray. She said yes. I prayed for "the wind to fall" followed by blowing out various wind sounds. I looked up and she was just staring at me in bewilderment and probably a little bit of nervousness.

I hope you don't think I'm being sacrilegious. It was all in good fun and from the initial reveal to this very day, every time I see her, we have a big laugh about it.

What does that story have to do with an eternal perspective? There are probably several analogies I could draw from it, but I want to key in on one. When I told her that her shoulder was going to be "a'ight," I was giving one of the key phrases of an eternal perspective, just not in proper English. You see, when we cultivate a posture that sees everything in light of eternity, we become convinced that everything is going to work out. And we are justified in being convinced of that truth. For the believer in Jesus Christ, all the junk, grief, difficulty, pressure, sin, and struggles we experience here are earth are temporary. They will not last. This is the journey, not the destination.

So, what is the potential problem? The danger lies in the fact that we can be dismissive and uncaring when people are going through difficulty. We can take our eternal perspective, apply it to everyday struggles people face, and basically tell them to get over it. We can lack compassion and sympathy for others. We can be devoid of care for those temporary trials because we are focused on the eternal glory that far outweighs it all. When that happens, we cease to be conduits for encouragement and can be perceived by others as harsh, judgmental, and insensitive.

Now, I am not saying that we should lay the eternal perspective aside and wallow with people in their despair, anxiety, fear, and doubt. We should help bring the light of eternity to the situation. We need to help people see the truth of the temporal and the eternal. However, the way we deliver that makes all the difference. In the moment of struggle it should not be forced with boldness, brashness, and bravado. It should be delivered with love, compassion and understanding.

That's the way Jesus did it.

Obviously, no one who ever walked this earth had a clearer eternal perspective than Jesus. After all, He *is* eternal. He had no beginning.

He has always been. There was that moment in time, 2000 years ago, when the Eternal One stepped out of eternity and became a man. But the Son did not begin in that moment, just His earthly life began. God the Father, God the Son, and God the Spirit are all One God and are all eternal. Jesus naturally sees things through the lens of eternity.

But that did not stop Him from being compassionate. Why did Jesus weep at the tomb of Lazarus? (John 11:35). Scholars debate it but we don't know for sure. It makes no sense that He would weep for Lazarus' death as He knew He was getting ready to raise Him. Was it because of the lack of faith of the ones around the tomb? That seems unlikely because He was getting ready to blow their minds. It could be because this miracle was not actually in Lazarus' best interest. Assuming Lazarus had faith in Jesus, he would have been in Paradise. Bringing him back to this sin-infested earth to die again would not have been ideal. Without knowing for sure, though, I think ultimately Jesus just loved the people who were grieving, and He grieved with them. He knew the outcome. He knew the glory that was getting ready to shine down. But He still cried with them.

Why did Jesus have compassion for the woman if He knew He was going to raise her son from the dead? (Luke 7:13). Why did He have compassion on the hungry crowd when He knew that the spiritual bread He offered was what they really needed? (Mark 8:2). Hebrews 4:14-16 states:

> *Since then we have a great high priest who has passed through the heavens, Jesus, the Son of God, let us hold fast our confession. For we do not have a high priest who is unable to sympathize with our weaknesses, but one who in every respect has been tempted as we are, yet without sin. Let us then with confidence draw near to the throne of grace, that we may receive mercy and find grace to help in time of need.*

Knowing the end from the beginning, He still cares for our daily struggles. Seeing the entirety of the story, He still sympathizes with our weaknesses. Fully understanding that everything is going to work out for the good to those whom He has called, He still beckons us to bring our hurts, failures, disappointments, and difficulties to Him.

So, we too, should be like Jesus. We point people to eternity and help them see temporal life through that lens. However, we love and care for people with a passion.

When we are committed to bearing one another's burdens and walking side by side through the temporal tribulations of this life, then we earn the platform to say confidently and compassionately, "It's gonna be a'ight."

CPSIA information can be obtained
at www.ICGtesting.com
Printed in the USA
LVHW010802240921
698637LV00005B/58